INCLINED TO
Liberty

THE FUTILE ATTEMPT TO SUPPRESS THE HUMAN SPIRIT

D1051934

LOUIS E. CARABINI

Ludwig
von Mises
Institute

AUBURN, ALABAMA

Copyright © 2008 by the Ludwig von Mises Institute

ISBN: 978-1-933550-29-9

To all who owed me nothing
and gave me everything

Contents

INTRODUCTION

IN THE FALL OF 2004, I had the pleasure of hosting several guests for a dinner party at my home, including a few professors from our local university. One professor I had never met, and another I'd encountered only briefly at a lecture he had given on Immanuel Kant. A friend of mine, who also was at the dinner that evening, knew both guests well, and had, in fact, warned me that they were sympathetic to socialism, and even Marxism. I knew he was eager to get us together since I had mentioned some time earlier that I would find an evening with a socialist quite exciting.

The evening was not a disappointment. After the customary delays of dinner and small talk, one professor fired the first salvo, and the fireworks commenced. Wine drowned any and all inhibitions. There is always much to consider and learn when strong-minded (yet friendly) adversaries challenge your core beliefs. The greatest lesson, at least for me, is not what takes place during a face-to-face argument, but later, when your adversaries' ideas nag at your own beliefs and force you to search for answers.

During that evening, I found myself reliving the past, especially when hearing such target words as "workers" and "capitalist." What I heard took me back about 40 years, to when I first found myself inclined to liberty. At that time, because the U.S. was in the midst of the Cold War with the Soviet Union, libertarian discussions often centered on communism. Although no one used words such as "proletariat" and "bourgeois" on the evening of my dinner, the references made that night to the poor and the rich reminded me of the historical Marxist class struggle between the downtrodden proletariats and the bourgeois property owners.

I actually believed that some of the more radical ideas proposed that evening had suffered their own mortal wounds, 13 years earlier, when in 1991 the world witnessed the supposed end of a human experiment that had tested the ideology of central planning and a policy of rigid authority over the lives of a large segment of humanity. This human experiment resulted in the death and suffering of countless millions. These caged people of Eastern Europe and Russia were never allowed to escape the confines of the laboratory until their restraining wall collapsed, and their bureaucracy imploded. The fallout of that disastrous experiment continues to this day.

While Marx's ideas were well-intentioned, if abstract, the unabashed use of a totalitarian state using his name did not represent an abstract economic textbook lesson, but rather a real, living example of how humans will act under rigid conditions. And, of course, the experiment was recent. One doesn't have to be an economist to know that there is a lesson to be learned from this seventy-year experiment, nor does one have to be a humanist to be horrified by the massive scale of suffering and death that resulted. I want to explore that lesson by analyzing the reasons why strategies that restrict human liberty must, by their very nature, fail, irrespective of their titles, purposes, or methods of engagement and administration.

I wish to thank and acknowledge David Gordon for his comments and encouragement after reading my first manuscript. I'm also thankful to Daniel Klein and Bruce Benson for their comments. Special thanks to David Hurwitz for scrutinizing and correcting several references. Very special thanks to Gloria Conner, who tirelessly edited every version of the manuscript, making numerous suggestions to help clarify my points. I remain responsible, of course, for all errors.

1

WHY WRITE THIS BOOK?

WHILE WRITING THIS BOOK, I often asked myself, "Why write this at all? Will I come up with such an unusual view and explanation of that view that someone with a socialist bent will, after reading it, suddenly exclaim, 'Oh! Now I concur'?" Hardly! Writing may not gain advocates, but it does help to codify one's own thoughts and beliefs, and that alone is rewarding.

I have often wondered why those with strong opinions about social affairs are always attracted toward one of two opposing poles. There are those *inclined to liberty*—freedom of the individual to live his or her life in any peaceful way. And there are those who are *inclined to mastery*—permitting others to live their lives only as another sees fit. It seems also that, once so inclined to one or the other of these philosophies, one is so inclined for life.

It is rare, in my experience, that people who align themselves with one camp or the other will, upon seeing some new evidence or hearing an argument contrary to their beliefs, switch camps. Why are some inclined to agree with, for example, a passage written by Milton Friedman, but disagree with one written by John Kenneth Galbraith, or the reverse? Perhaps we carry genes that predispose us to one inclination and render us immune to contrary evidence.

So why debate if we are so firmly predisposed? There seems to be a spirit within us that wants to convert others to our beliefs without having to assess the real value of such conversions. After all, what one person believes does not obstruct the beliefs of another. If one converts a socialist to a libertarian or an atheist to a Christian, or vice versa, what is gained? Maybe the gain is simply the comfort we experience when someone else reconfirms that our beliefs are "correct" after all.

Whatever the case, the dinner party that evening led to my own personal search for answers and, ultimately, the writing of this book, a most rewarding venture that I would never have undertaken had it not been for the views expressed by my guests that night. I thank them, and my friend Don De Francisco, in particular, for having made that experience possible.[1]

---

[1]For those inclined to the culinary arts, the fare that evening included barbecued rack of lamb garnished with garlic and rosemary, roasted red peppers, broccoli, *penne alla checca* (penne pasta, fresh tomatoes, basil, and garlic), and several bottles of California, French, and Italian wines.

2

THE PROPOSITIONS OF THAT EVENING

SOME OF THE PROPOSITIONS offered during that lively evening were:

"No one should be allowed to own a yacht."

"The salaries of company executives are too high."

"No one should be allowed to inherit wealth."

But the statement that I found most intriguing, and the one that initially drove me to write, was:

"It is not fair that companies can terminate their workers just to increase profits."

However, as I thought of a suitable response, I realized that this proposition was no different in principle from the others. While some statements were more radical than others, each basically contains a notion that something is unfair and that we ought to do something to right that unfairness by instituting prohibitions.

Reading these "is" and "ought" notions into the propositions, the statements then become:

"It is unfair that someone can earn much more than another, so *we* ought to prohibit people from earning that much."

"It is unfair that someone can own a yacht, so *we* ought to prohibit such ownership."

"It is unfair that someone can bequeath wealth to an heir, so *we* ought to disallow such transfers of wealth."

"It is unfair that an employer can terminate workers just to increase profits, so *we* ought to prohibit employers from doing so."

The "we" in each of these cases is the royal "we"—that is, the State. The royal "we" connotes a moral justification for physically forcing others to live their lives as the personal "I" sees fit. Imagine how alarming these propositions would sound if the personal "I" were used instead of the abstract and justifiable royal "we." For instance:

"The salaries of executives are too high, so *I* will personally threaten to incarcerate any executive who accepts a salary and any company owner who pays a salary higher than what *I* think is reasonable."

"*I* will incarcerate anyone who buys, builds, or sells a yacht that *I* consider too large and luxurious."

Any prohibition by the State also implies incarceration or death if refusal to comply is carried to its ultimate end. Although incarceration and death hide behind each proposition mentioned that evening, the clear realization of such physical punishments comes to the forefront when we substitute "I" for "we." The royal "we" seems to moralize and justify acts that the "I" would render reprehensible.

3

BLAME AND RESENTMENT

BENEATH THIS NOTION OF unfairness and the obligation to right it are the implications of fault and contempt. There is an unspoken, but very real, contempt for the rich yacht owner, contempt for the factory owner, contempt for the executive—in other words, a general contempt for wealthy people. Today, there is an outpouring of contempt in the media for the drug companies, the oil companies, and the Wal-Marts of the world. In a nutshell, each proposition made at that evening's dinner painted a picture of a villain, a victim, and an emancipator—in other words, the rich, the poor, and the proponent of those propositions (with the help of the State), respectively.

The message implied in each proposition is not simply that "the poor are too poor and the rich are too rich." The very heart of each of the propositions is that the cause of the poor being too poor is that the rich are too rich. In one sense, we are told that the "haves" are at fault for preventing the "have-nots" from gaining wealth, and, in another sense, that if the "haves" had less, the "have-nots" would have more by default. The evidence shows that both these assertions are fallacious.

Expressions such as "filthy rich," "selfish rich," and "greedy rich" exhibit a deeply rooted resentment of the rich. As Robert Solomon explains, "Through resentment we make it sound as though we are lucky not to have those things that we want but don't have. We feel self-righteous precisely because we are not rich."[2] Jean-Paul Sartre said that resentment is an act by which we escape responsibility for a world that we find too difficult to accept. Still worse, resentment can give way to *schadenfreude*—taking joy in other people's suffering. This vindictive form of resentment is revealed in statements such as, "They finally got what was coming," relative to the news that someone wealthy has had a setback.

---

[2]Robert Solomon, *The Passions: Philosophy and the Intelligence of Emotions*, Lecture 8 (The Teaching Company, 2006).

4

IN A WORLD OF INEQUALITY, ARE THERE REALLY VILLAINS AND VICTIMS?

IN A WORLD IN which economic inequalities are universal, why do so many envision the existence of villains and victims? Does this view stem from a belief that there is a static quantity of wealth or resources in the world, and when someone gets more than an equal share, someone else must receive less? Or does the view stem from a belief that rich people have garnered their wealth undeservingly, by unscrupulous, greedy, or inconsiderate behavior? Or does it stem from envy, resentment, or simply a blatant attempt to increase one's own status by decreasing that of another?

For many, possibly most, such villain/victim assertions do not stem from any deep reasoning. The ideas are simply a regurgitation of what they have read and heard in the news. Spewing the words and ideas of others is particularly likely when one belongs to a political, social, religious, or racial camp. Camp leaders, especially political ones, appear in the news daily, damning their adversarial camp leaders with senseless headline-grabbing charges designed to excite their followers and, hopefully, capture a few more gullible camp converts.

For those who join a camp, the spokesperson becomes similar to kin, and those in opposing camps automatically become foes; the people involved resemble participants in a feud. No matter what the kin says, those in the camp will accept it and despise whatever the foe advocates. It's easier to become a parrot when aligned with any group, be it political, social, religious, or racial, than to think for oneself. Regardless of the type of group, the spokesperson will tell the crowd what they want to hear.

Crowds gather to support their kin and maybe pick up another malicious one-liner to put in their quiver to shoot mindlessly at the next foe they encounter. Unless one is critical and truly considers whether the spokesperson's statements actually make sense, one may likely continue to advocate policies that would produce the very opposite of what one actually desires. Rent control laws, drug and alcohol prohibitions, and government subsidies are just a few examples where such policies produced the opposite of their desired goals.

5

THE THEM VS. US SYNDROME

DURING THE 2004 PRESIDENTIAL campaign, one candidate decried, "Two Americas: One privileged, the other burdened. One America that does the work, another that reaps the reward. One America that pays the taxes, another America that gets the tax breaks."[3]

Demagogic statements like these simply are pleas to the masses: "Vote for me, and I'll get you your fair share of wealth, by taking it from those who have more than you. Vote for me, and I'll rob Peter (that's them) to pay Paul (that's us)." Pitting the rich against the poor is only one of the many foot-stomping campaign themes based on the mind-set of "them versus us." Self-appointed leaders pit white people against black people, men against women, factory owners against workers, foreigners against Americans, and new immigrants against descendants of older ones. Blaming one group for the ills of another is a sure way to provoke and sustain ill will between the groups.

Following these Pied Pipers of divisive protest and their pipe dreams is a good way to ensure that you never get what they promise or what you desire. Blaming others for what we don't have

---

[3]According to the Internal Revenue Service, more than 50 percent of the tax revenue in 2002 came from the top 5 percent of the taxpayers (up from 43.6 percent in 1990), 80 percent came from the top 25 percent, and virtually all (96 percent) of the tax revenue came from the top 50 percent. The IRS data refute the candidate's implication that the rich pay little tax.

directs our energy and ingenuity away from the only reliably effective source of achievement in the world—self-reliance. Once we realize that no one owes us a life free of misery, we actually begin to search for real remedies instead of wasting time and energy accusing others of causing our woes and expecting restitution.

Every U.S. election campaign is a tug-of-war between Robin Hoods, each accusing the other of either giving too little and taking too much or taking too little and giving too much. People get angry about their every grievance because they are constantly bombarded with the notion that they are the victims of someone's plot to take an unfair advantage of them.

With such stories constantly in the news, it's easy to develop a conspiracy complex or even paranoia about anything we don't like by blaming it on someone else "getting away with murder." If gasoline prices are too high, blame the oil companies. If drug prices are too high, blame the drug companies. Tomorrow it will be a different scapegoat, someone new who owes us a free this or a cheaper that. Just stay tuned and our Congressman or news reporter will give us the latest culprit in vogue. The bumper sticker "Corporate Greed vs. Human Need" exemplifies this kind of paranoia.

In a democratic society in which everyone has a say about everyone else's lifestyle, it's no wonder we spend so much time debating one man's pet peeve and another's grand solution. In a self-reliant society, pet peeves may keep us awake at night, but in a democratic society, we can spend a lifetime of energy creating one pet peeve after another and offering "our" solution, because we now have a voice. Of course, who doesn't want to be heard, particularly when we know that someone with political power over others will listen? So the "them vs. us" notion permeates the news and becomes the publicized rationale for new legislation, and yes, may even alter our own thinking, if we ignore common sense.

Consider one of the most horrific "them vs. us" political campaigns in recent history: the Jewish "them" versus the Aryan "us" campaign waged in Germany in the 1930s and 1940s. Many were led to believe that Jews were a detriment to society and that a fair and just solution (named *Endlösung der Judenfrage* [The Final Solution of the Jewish Question]) was to isolate and eradicate them.

6

Painting Mental Images

Envision what comes to mind when we hear, as stated that evening at my dinner party, that companies fire workers *just to increase profits*. The statement invites us to picture poor workers and their families living at the mercy of a greedy employer. And now, jobless, those workers will no longer be able to maintain even the meager standard of living to which they have become accustomed. This sad and exploitive "picture" is embellished by envisioning the employer as an ogre who has pushed his workers out onto the street *just to increase profits*, without regard for their suffering.

In a flash, the mind creates mental pictures produced by these types of phrases and, depending on our political or social stance, these images can erupt into a quick visceral reaction, with such responses as, "There ought to be a law!" or "How can one be so cruel!" We paint these pictures, using the philosophical, political, or religious brush of our leanings. Then, we convey the mental pictures to others with personal coloring. Every day we are inundated with stories, often distorted, by the media. We develop meticulous mental pictures from these stories, with very little understanding of the circumstances surrounding, or leading up to, them.

The baseless, albeit vivid, mental images harbored by supporters of Germany's reign of terror during the 1930s and 1940s helped pave the way to "justify" the deaths of six million Jews and the suffering of millions more. History is replete with human gullibility; countless rulers have swayed their followers into believing that their economic problems have been caused by someone else's race, ethnicity, religion, or economic status. Unfortunately, attempts to trigger these baseless mental images are not limited to only rulers and political aspirants.

Television reporters are very adept at delivering punchy sound and visual bites that can trigger unfounded mental images. As gas prices rose in the spring of 2006, TV networks went hunting for "victims" and aired 183 statements from upset or beleaguered gasoline buyers.[4] *ABC World News Tonight* showcased a woman who claimed she had to pawn her wedding set to put gas in her husband's truck. A week later, *CBS Evening News* suggested that higher pump prices meant the elderly were going to starve: "They're used to living on fixed incomes, but now, skyrocketing gas prices are forcing seniors to make difficult choices. Some are cutting back on gasoline; others say they're eating less." *The Nightly News* showed a California man filling up his pick-up truck. "$3.41," he groused. "They should start handing out knives to cut your arm and leg off."

The reporters left no doubt about who the villains were. On *ABC Good Morning America*, Diane Sawyer reported: "Pain at the pump. Oil companies are getting ready to raise prices again. Is it time to turn the tables and tax their record profits?" Three days later, her colleague Charlie Gibson announced: "Pain at the pump. The big oil companies report billions in profits. Is our pain their gain?" *The CBS Evening News* opened with this indictment: "Gas price gouging. I'm Sharyl Attkisson with what Congress is— and is not—doing about it."

Such antibusiness stories fill newspapers, talk shows, and television news programs. Many have even worked their way into movies. As we read and hear more of these distorted stories, we

---

[4]Media Research Center, "Media Reality Check," May 4, 2006.

eventually begin to believe that there must be a vindictive villain behind everything we don't like. We hear that a drug company has just discovered a cure for a horrible disease—but the next day we hear that the company charges far too much for a pill that costs very little to produce. Yes, that *second* pill rolling off the factory production line may cost pennies to produce, but that second pill would never have been manufactured unless the pharmaceutical company had spent millions of dollars to produce the first one. As for oil companies: if gouging us with higher gasoline prices is their way of making record profits, then why stop at only $4 a gallon? Why not make a real killing and charge $10, or better yet, $100 per gallon?

Attacking profits as a means to lower prices is the very opposite of what political leaders and news commentators should do. Grand profits are the most effective means to lower prices, since they attract investors and entrepreneurs to a business that they would otherwise overlook. The resulting competition and innovative technology arising from this new interest underlie the process that brings us an endless stream of goods and services at the most attractive prices.

When questioning the prices of goods, we cannot ignore the fact that prices reflect relationships between the perceived values of two objects: money and goods. Price changes are simply changes in those relationships. When we say that a good is higher in price, we mean that it now takes more money to get it. But we could just as well say that the money is lower in "price," since it now takes fewer such goods to get it. Thus, to determine if something is truly more expensive now than in the past, we must include in our considerations the value of money.

Derry Brownfield offers this clever illustration to describe the relationship between money and gasoline:

> I began a recent presentation before a large group of cattle producers (R-CALFUSA) by showing a paper dollar bill and a silver coin. The words "one dollar" is inscribed on both the coin and the paper, yet the paper dollar will only pay for about one quart of gasoline at today's prices, while the silver dollar will

pay for well over five gallons. I explained to my audience that consumer prices are not high—the paper dollar has lost most of its value. It makes no difference how high the price of gasoline goes, a silver dollar will continue to buy gas for 20 cents a gallon, exactly the price gas was during the Great Depression. Based on 1940 prices, a paper dollar is worth about two pennies.[5]

No one owes us gasoline, medicine, food, jobs, or anything else, so why should we criticize the person for the price he charges or the wage he offers for something that he was not obligated to provide us in the first place? It would make more sense to criticize the grocer for not selling us cheaper gasoline or medicine than it would to criticize those who *are* offering to sell them at all. When we consider all the goods and services provided by those who have chosen to do so, we can only be thankful for their voluntary contributions to the betterment of our lives.

When reading and listening to the barrage of antibusiness news stories, we can easily be led, if we are not careful, to paint the mental image that anyone who makes money—as long as it's the other guy—is never as wise, fair, moral, compassionate, or deserving as we are.

---

[5]Derry Brownfield, "Silver, Gold and the IRS," NewsWithViews, June 5, 2008. http://www.newswithviews.com/brownfield/brownfield67.htm.

7

SMALL GROUPS VS. LARGE GROUPS

A COMMON ECONOMIC ERROR when assessing the effect of a social event or a proposed action is the failure to account for all effects—current and future, obvious and not-so-obvious. In a small setting, it is easy to envision all the effects of an action, thereby giving a proposal a more accurate evaluation. Reasoning and common sense (intuition) can be valuable tools when predicting the outcome of a proposed policy or event within a small group. However, such tools become far less reliable when assessing outcomes in larger groups. When we interact with others in small groups, our instincts, for the most part, tell us without much deliberation, that we can achieve our goals with less effort and conflict when the means to those goals align with "the Golden Rule." In a family, neighborhood, company, business relationship, or similar small group, most of us will adopt "the Golden Rule" as our guide. However, we tend to abandon that concept when it comes to a large political group.

Should a neighbor need help, we would never consider going around the neighborhood threatening those who do not pitch in. We instinctively understand that charity is voluntary, and we are generally eager to help when we see someone in need. In a small setting, we view the use of force as a means to help others to be the antithesis of charity. However, in a political arena, we find ourselves condoning, even promoting, the use of physical force as the proper means to extract aid. And when such force is used, we paradoxically refer to it as an act of charity and compassion.

Virtue and cooperation are instinctive codes of conduct that have evolved over time because they provide mechanisms for survival and reproduction superior to those based on a code of coercion.[5] Since our hunter-gatherer ancestors lived in small groups, generally fewer than fifty members, for millions of years, our inherited common-sense instincts are not as keen when large groups are involved. An act that one would consider reprehensible and nonsensical if conducted in a small group may become quite acceptable in a large setting, because our brains are not as adept at sensing and evaluating large group interaction.

---

[5]Matt Ridley, *The Origins of Virtue: Human Instincts and the Evolution of Cooperation* (New York: Viking Penguin, 1996). Also see Robert Wright, *The Moral Animal: Why We Are the Way We Are* (New York: Vintage Books, 1994).

8

Manna from Heaven?

If you think health care is expensive now, wait until it's free.
- P.J. O'Rourke

If wishes were horses, beggars would ride.
-Proverb

THE NOTION THAT ONE man's need is another man's obligation has become so engrained in people's minds that revolutions, riots, and demonstrations erupt almost weekly around the world. People routinely blame their political leaders for not providing them better lifestyles. Many believe that the State can miraculously provide prosperity for everyone simply by creating and distributing wealth. People see the State as the source of a "free lunch"—manna from heaven. Not surprisingly, nearly every prospective political leader reinforces this "free lunch." Political candidates tempt voters with an assortment of freebies, and then, when elected, add those offerings to all those freebies already on the table.

As P.J. O'Rourke quips above, the most expensive lunch is a free one. In the real world, someone must work to provide and pay for all the free benefits that others receive—and that "someone" isn't the State. States only provide what they acquire by directly taxing those who are hard at work producing real goods, and indirectly taxing everyone—including retirees—by issuing fiat money.[6] States can also use borrowed money, but doing so only increases the State's future dependency on direct and indirect taxes to repay those lenders. The degree and amount of such manipulation and skullduggery boggle the mind. It is virtually impossible for anyone to calculate the actual dollar cost of all these "free lunches." The greatest travesty, however, is not the up-front taxes, but rather the detrimental impact on the recipients of the free lunches. These are the very people we intend to help, but who are instead enticed into a dependency trap.

---

[6]Fiat refers to making something so by decree—in this case, money. Governments create fiat money by printing currency and by issuing bank credit.

9

THE FALSE LURE
OF DEMOCRACY

It is a poor mind that will think with the multitude because it is a multitude: truth is not altered by the opinions of the vulgar or the confirmation of the many. It is more blessed to be wise in truth in face of opinion than to be wise in opinion in face of truth.[7]

-Giordano Bruno (1548–1600)

SOME MIGHT ARGUE THAT a few of the propositions made that evening at dinner originated in Never-Never Land, because they seem too far-fetched to be entertained seriously. But are they, in principle, so different from the outcries we continually hear from political candidates, the news media, and special interest groups? The idea that one should not be allowed to own a yacht, as was proposed at dinner, is no different in principle from the 1990 luxury tax imposed on yacht purchases. Both deny people the freedom to spend their earnings as they wish. The idea that an employer should not be allowed to terminate an employee to make a profit, as was also proposed at dinner, is similar to the numerous federal and state restrictions that currently deny employers the freedom to manage their businesses in a way they deem most profitable.

The very essence of democracy encourages everyone to express opinions about human activities that are none of their

---

[7] James Lewis McIntyre, *Giordano Bruno* (New York: Macmillan, 1903), p. 50.

business. There are few days that someone doesn't ask me what I think that "we" (the royal "we") should "do" about this or that individual, organization, or group activity that is clearly neither my business nor theirs. It is not the answers to such questions that should give us concern; the mere *asking* has become so common-place—and with such a sense of democratic pride and entitle-ment—that today nearly every aspect of human activity is con-sidered public domain.

In a democracy, each of us has license to prescribe for others how to live their lives; run their businesses; whom they may hire; what wages they may pay; what prices they may charge; what, where, when, and how much they may buy or sell; what they may teach; what and where they may smoke, drink, and eat; what they may plant; what medicines they may take; what houses they may build and where they may build them; what they may say; how and where they may practice their religion (even what religion); where they may go; where they may live; how they may die; with whom and how they may engage in sex; whom they may marry and with whom they may associate. On and on this intrusion goes, with more "dos" and "don'ts" added every day.

A staggering 78,851 pages of newly proposed regulations were posted in the *2004 U.S. Federal Register*, the government's official daily publication for rules, proposed rules, notices, and executive orders. An even more staggering fact: that annual number is about average for the past ten years. Federal regulations, com-bined with others from state and local governments, have reached the point where virtually every human act is subject to some kind of scrutiny by a governmental agency.

While many of these regulations are adopted at the urging of self-righteous do-gooders imposing their social and moral values on the rest of us, other regulations are adopted at the urging of organizations that seek entitlements, special privileges, and cur-tailment of competition. Labor unions, farmers, and other perma-nent lobbies, such as AARP, are exceptionally skilled at pushing their special privileges through Congress.[8] In 2005, there were

---

[8]Center for Responsive Politics, a nonpartisan organization, reported federal political contributions of $1.6 billion during 2006. Labor unions reported

34,785 registered lobbyists in Washington, D.C.—more than double the number from just five years earlier.[9] Businesses and other entities engage these experts to introduce legislation, manipulate regulations, and obtain special favors that prevent, subdue, or overcome competition.

In the spirit of "fair trade," there are 8,757 tariffs and numerous quotas on imports into the U.S.[10] Tariffs penalize consumers by forcing them to pay higher prices for foreign and domestic goods than would otherwise exist in a free-trade market. These higher prices when paid to a domestic producer are equivalent to subsidies. There are also government subsidies paid directly to manufacturers and farmers to overcome foreign competition. Farm subsidies alone reached $177 billion from 1995 to 2006.[11] According to the *Farmers Weekly Report*, nearly 70 percent of U.S. soybean value now comes from the U.S. government in the form of subsidies. As can be expected, this unintended but lucrative incentive has caused a 25 percent increase in soybean planting in the U.S. since 1998. As evidenced by their sheer abundance, quotas, tariffs, and subsidies are especially easy to obtain in a democratic republic where one need only persuade one or two politicians. The "you vote for mine and I'll vote for yours" Congressional buddy system takes care of the rest of the process.

With every president, senator, congressional representative, governor, and assemblyman trying to make a historical impact on society, it's no wonder we have an unrelenting flood of new "laws" (more accurately, legislations) enacted every year. Today, virtually every activity is subject to local, state, or federal regulation. During the 2006 California legislative session, there were 4,929 bills

---

$66 million; AARP reported $23.2 million; and agribusiness reported $88.6 million in political contributions during 2006.

[9]Jeffrey H. Birnbaum, "The Road to Riches Is Called K Street—Lobbying Firms Hire More, Pay More, Charge More to Influence Government," *Washington Post*, 22 June 2005.

[10]James Bovard, *The Fair Trade Fraud, How Congress Pillages the Consumer and Decimates American Competitiveness* (New York: St. Martin's Press, 1991), p. 7.

[11]Environmental Working Group, 2006 *Farm Subsidy*. http://farm.ewg.org/farm/region.php?fips=00000.

written (1,853 in the Senate and 3,076 in the Assembly); 1,172 were passed, and the governor vetoed only 262. On the final day of that session, the Assembly speaker proudly announced, "I think this is going to be a landmark legislative year for us."

Regulations are very likely a greater impediment to freedom and prosperity than are imposed taxes. As with the imposition of taxes, regulations divert human energy from productive actions to nonproductive actions. As such, society loses the otherwise meaningful production of those bureaucrats involved in the creation and enforcement of regulations, the professional consultants who assist those being regulated, and, to some degree, those to whom the regulations actually apply. Virtually every major U.S. company has a cadre of lawyers, accountants, and consultants who ferret through the perpetually changing labyrinth of regulations to identify those that are applicable to their clientele, interpret their meaning, and then recommend operational adjustments to those clients.

This ever-increasing burden of regulations, however, is predictably met with human perseverance and ingenuity. Human nature will find innovative ways to circumvent the full impact of these bureaucratic restrictions. Many people discover loopholes that require less inconvenience than would compliance, others operate at the regulatory fringe where the ability to enforce compliance is unclear, or they simply operate entirely outside the regulatory arm of the State. All the energy thus diverted from productive activity into meeting or circumventing regulatory compliance simply reduces the production of real goods and services, thereby increasing their end cost to consumers.

A democratic state will naturally gravitate to an ever-greater "tragedy of the commons,"[12] in which citizens try to get a bigger

---

[12]Garrett Hardin popularized the concept "the tragedy of the commons" in an article published by *Science* in 1968. However, the concept can be traced back to Aristotle, who said: "For that which is common to the greatest number has the least care bestowed upon it. Every one thinks chiefly of his own, hardly at all of the common interest; and only when he is himself concerned as an individual" (*Politics*, 1261, b34).

share of the funds acquired by the State. Since those funds are now commonly owned, everyone has a right to claim a share. Even free riders become just as deserving of shares as do society's contributors. Instead of being ostracized, free riders are now *entitled* to free rides. These entitlements are further justified by their advocates declaring them as "rights" (active rights), implying they have equal footing with natural rights (passive, or inalienable rights). An active right is a claim upon the life of another, while a natural right obligates others to refrain from any such claims. Therefore, a claimant of a right to a free ride, such as free health care, is a disclaimer of the natural, inalienable rights of the person upon whom the claim is made.[13] Frédéric Bastiat (1801–1850), the famous French political economist, described the state as the great fiction by which everybody tries to live at the expense of everybody else.

This is not meant to cast blame on those who exploit the democratic system to obtain favors and resources. It is only rational to acquire resources at the least perceived cost. The democratic State simply provides an attractive means for some to acquire the resources produced by others at little or no cost to themselves, while preventing any real recourse for those from whom those resources are taken. Individuals who take resources from others without the strong arm of the State behind them would find it a risky and expensive enterprise.

When the opportunity to punish (ostracize) free riders is absent, the highest producers and contributors to the community typically ratchet back their own contributions to something near

---

[13]I do not imply that there are natural rights, since such rights make little sense to me even though many libertarians base their endorsement of liberty on them. Natural rights imply a privilege that others are obliged to respect. One's life is one's sole responsibility, as is the gaining of respect for it. An ideal way to gain respect for one's life and property is to respect the life and property of others. The "rights" card is often played as a trump card when we are unable to persuade others by reason or unable to get what we desire by cooperative means. Furthermore, demanding respect for natural rights arguably (and dangerously) invites others to demand equal respect for any of their perceived rights.

the group average.[14] This iterative ratchet effect was demonstrated in many natural experiments that occurred in the former Soviet Union. Soviet agricultural policies nationalized farmland and forced farmers to organize their labor as a collective action. Still, the Soviets allowed 3 percent of the land on collective farms to be held privately, so local farming families could produce food for their own consumption and privately sell any excess. This private land produced an estimated one-third of all agricultural products in the Soviet Union.[15] These small plots saved many Russians from famine. In China, the greatest famine in human history followed the collectivization of all peasant land. Statistics indicate that at least thirty million people starved to death from 1958 to 1962.[16]

The periods of famine following collectivized farming exemplify "the tragedy of the commons," in which each person receives the same share of the total production, regardless of individual productive contribution. The Pilgrims experienced this same tragedy of the commons during the first few years of arriving in America, when their crop production was delivered to a common pool. Facing another disastrous year of crop production and famine, they decided to parcel the land in 1623; each family was rewarded with what they produced. As a result, the Pilgrims celebrated their first bountiful crop in the very same year the plan was adopted.[17]

---

[14]Ernst Fehr and Simon Gachter, "Cooperation and Punishment in Public Goods Experiments," *American Economic Review* 90, no. 4 (2000): 980–94.

[15]C.A. Knox Lovell, "The Role of Private Subsidiary Farming during the Soviet Seven-Year Plan, 1959–65," *Soviet Studies* 20, no. 1 (1968): 46–66.

[16]J. Becker, *Hungry Ghosts: Mao's Secret Famine* (New York: Free Press, 1997).

[17]Gary Galles, "Property and the First Thanksgiving," 2004, http://www.mises.org/story/1678; Benjamin Powell, "The Pilgrims' Real Thanksgiving Lesson," *Charlotte Observer* and *The San Diego Union-Tribune*, 25 November 2004.

10

WEALTH BEGETS WEALTH

THOSE WHO EARN WEALTH by producing goods and services that others choose to purchase have freed multitudes from the miseries that nature would have otherwise bestowed upon them. To earn wealth, one must offer goods and services that others consider more valuable than the price at which those goods and services are being offered.[18] One who produces and sells a million widgets to a million different people at a one dollar profit per widget becomes a millionaire. But each of the million people who buys that product gains—through the purchase of a widget—something greater than its cost. Why? Well, if the value of the widget were *not* considered greater than what was paid for it, then the buyer would not have purchased the widget. The amount of gain is individually subjective, but if each purchaser perceives the added benefit of the purchase to be at least one dollar, all purchasers, as a group, would have gained at least $1 million in wealth.

Because the earning of wealth in free markets is dependent upon those who perceive value in the earner's goods and services,

---

[18]Wealth gained from voluntary exchanges is earned, whereas wealth gained from embezzlement, extortion, theft, or other such involuntary means is, instead, a form of takings.

the greater the wealth *earned* by one necessitates the greater the perceived wealth (well-being) *gained* by another. This necessary bilateral gain in wealth also applies to the exchange of labor and wages. The value of one's labor is worth less than the wages to the employee, and more than the wages to the employer. Thus, both the employee and employer are wealthier with the exchange than without the exchange.

Of course, values at the time of an exchange may not always turn out to be as originally perceived. Buying a car that turns out to be a "lemon," regretting the purchase of that last drink, buying a stock that later plummets, or taking a job that is less rewarding than originally thought are a few examples. Nevertheless, *at the time* of a voluntary exchange, each party perceives the exchange as a gain in well-being.

When we visualize money flowing from one person to another, we tend to focus on the gain of the seller, not the gain of the buyer. Even governments seem to focus on the gain of the seller by reporting a negative balance of trade for the country that buys goods from a foreign country and a positive balance of trade when it sells goods to them. Yet, when we personally buy something—a new car, computer, suit, or dress—we are more excited about the purchase we have made than we are about the money we used to make that purchase. The very word "trade" implies a voluntary exchange, and therefore, a resulting "positive" for each side of the transaction.

Reported U.S. trade imbalances of deficits and surpluses are fictitious, since no trade would have occurred if either party saw that trade as a deficit. Only by failing to account for all transfers of money for services and investments among trading entities can one fabricate an imbalance of trade. If I buy a loaf of bread from the grocer across the street, we would not call it an imbalance of trade, that is, a positive for the grocer and a negative for me. However, if the street were the border between the U.S. and Canada, my purchase would be considered a deficit for the U.S. and a surplus for Canada in a balance of trade calculation.

11

MONEY—WHAT IS IT?

SINCE ALL OF THE propositions at that eventful dinner relate to money, let's look at what money really is. Today, governments monopolize money, but this was not always the case. Money emerged as a medium of exchange to facilitate the trading of goods when the division of labor replaced self-sufficiency and bartering became impractical because of the increasing variety of available goods and services. Various forms of money evolved that sellers were willing to accept in lieu of someone else's goods or services. Some of those early forms of money were seashells, tobacco, salt, spices, and metals.

In a society without money, each producer would have to find a complementary producer with whom to exchange goods and services directly. With money as an intermediary, a producer needs only to find someone who wants his goods or services. The time devoted to searching for a person with a coincidence of wants in a barter market can now, with money, be devoted instead to the production of more goods and services.

To illustrate the utility of money, let's say John produces eggs, and Bob produces wheat. If John wants wheat from Bob, but Bob doesn't want John's eggs, John could give Bob a facilitator—for instance, nails—for his wheat. Bob, in turn, could trade the nails for milk if the dairyman doesn't want his wheat. The dairyman could then use nails to obtain eggs from John. The ability to trade indirectly using money provides each person the opportunity to get his preferred choice. In this case, John gets his wheat, Bob gets his milk, and the dairyman gets his eggs.

In a volitional exchange, each party values what is received more than what is given up. In other words, when Bob accepts nails for his wheat, he is valuing that quantity of nails greater than the quantity of wheat that he gives John. Conversely, John places greater value on the quantity of wheat than on the quantity of nails.

In a similar scenario, John could give Bob an IOU for a specific quantity of eggs instead of giving Bob nails. As before, Bob doesn't want eggs, but he accepts John's IOU in exchange for the wheat because he knows that the quantity of eggs the IOU represents has value to others. Bob then uses John's IOU in exchange for milk from the dairyman. The IOU can continue to be used in further exchanges until someone redeems it, simply by going to John and getting the eggs, at which time the IOU is voided.

The willingness to accept John's IOU depends on John's reputation. The more reputable John is, the more readily his IOUs will be accepted. If John defaults on his IOU, his reputation will suffer, and, as a result, he may be relegated to trading his eggs only by direct barter with someone who can actually use the eggs. Let's say John always honors his IOUs, so that everyone who requests redemption gets a full quantity of eggs. In time, John's IOUs become so popular that only a few ever cash them in for actual eggs. At this point, John may be tempted to write more IOUs than the quantity of eggs he is capable of producing to meet all the outstanding IOUs. John does so, and finds that he can write about four times as many IOUs as he possesses in eggs at any given time.

The system appears to work well, since everyone who wants to redeem IOUs gets eggs. John is living a more prosperous lifestyle— actually a lifestyle about four times better than before, since he has garnered four times the goods from others than he was able to get before. Since John is enjoying life to a greater extent than his productive contribution to the community warrants, the rest of the community must, by deduction, be enjoying life to a lesser extent than the sum of their productive contributions.

As John's IOUs become more popular as a medium of exchange, fewer people find the need to redeem them. So John increases the ratio of IOUs to his production of eggs until there are literally one-hundred IOUs for every dozen eggs. John is now living a great life of splendor, yet contributes little to the community. The community is not wealthier with all those unredeemed IOUs circulating about, since no one is eating the eggs represented by those IOUs. Even when the members of the community realize that John can't possibly honor all his IOUs, they continue accepting them in trade for their goods, believing the next person in line will accept them, as well.

Eventually, John drops the use of the word "eggs" on his IOUs to prevent even those few who may want to redeem them for actual eggs from doing so, or to thwart a possible "egg run." Like other goods, as the number of IOUs in the community increases, their exchange value decreases. Whereas at one time an IOU for a dozen eggs could attain a gallon of milk, now it will only attain a fraction of a cup of that same milk.

Well, by now you may be thinking, "John behaves just like the government." Not quite. Only if John were to prevent others in the community from competing with him and forcibly require everyone in the community to accept his IOUs in payment of all debts would his actions be equivalent to those of government. In a free market, money like John's IOUs would encounter more and more competition long before it would reach the inflationary level described above. As confidence in the issuer of an IOU fades, competitors seize upon the opportunity. All the new competitors try to reassure those who accept their IOUs that theirs, unlike John's, are backed by something real and redeemable.

No government today issues money that is redeemable for anything of value. U.S. dollars were, at one time, IOUs redeemable for gold. But when more and more money was printed with no commensurate addition to the supply of gold, the government was compelled to prevent redemption to avoid a "run" on its gold supply. In 1933, the U.S. government simply declared the ownership of gold by U.S. citizens illegal, in effect, reneging on its earlier promise of redemption. Then, in 1971, the government had to renege on the redemption in gold for the dollars held by foreign entities, as well. Since then, there has been nothing redeemable for a U.S. dollar; it is deemed money by edict, and must be accepted to satisfy any debt.[19]

As we've seen, one who issues an IOU without the ability to meet its full redemption enjoys the fruits of the labor of others without working and contributing to the welfare of the community. In the above example, John, the issuer of unbacked IOUs, is a free rider, getting a benefit without a cost. Governments are no different. Their issuance of money by edict (fiat) is simply another form of taking, akin to taxes and tariffs.

As governments issue greater quantities of fiat money, the unit value of that money continually falls, harming primarily those with savings and, in particular, the elderly, who have saved their earnings for retirement. The money that they have worked most of their lives to save has depreciated to such an extent that many cannot afford to retire.

Due to inflation's devastating effect on the elderly, the process of increasing the fiat money supply is the most insidious form of taxation. Absent any inflation of currency, goods in general would fall in price because of new technology and competition, thereby giving one's savings more purchasing power and making one's plans for retirement more feasible.

---

[19]The Continental Congress first authorized the printing of fiat currency to finance the American Revolution. Without gold or silver backing, the continental dollar quickly became worthless. Thus, the expression "not worth a Continental" came into vogue.

12

MONEY IS NOT PROSPERITY

WHILE MONEY INCREASES THE efficiency of trading goods and services, money in itself does not create prosperity. Prosperity is created by producing goods and services that people value. If the U.S. government printed and distributed $1 million to every household in the country (approximately $100 trillion), would we all live better lives? If the answer is "yes," why not do even better by having the government print and hand out $1 billion per household? You probably sense something is wrong with that suggestion, but what is it?

Let's examine the assumption that money equals prosperity by viewing a society of five people. In this society, there is production, trading, and money. For simplicity's sake, let's say each member produces 20 units of a different good during a given period and each member's unit of goods has a similar subjective value to each of the other members. As it stands, the society's prosperity (wealth) is then 100 (5 x 20) units of goods. Let's say we give each member $1,000. Irrespective of the additional money, the total quantity of the community's wealth remains at 100 units of goods, with each member contributing 20 units to that overall level of wealth. Even if we were to give each member $1 million there would still only exist 100 units produced—in other words, no increase in prosperity. In the first example, each unit of goods might equate to, say, $50; however, in the second example, each unit of goods could equate to $50,000.

During Germany's hyperinflation in the 1920s, a millionaire was actually a pauper. Government printing presses were working at full capacity, twenty-four hours a day. The famous caricature of a person hauling his money in a wheelbarrow exemplified the worthlessness of the German mark in 1923. In 1914, the mark was backed by gold and had a value equal to one quarter of a U.S. dollar. By 1923, the mark's value was one trillionth that of a U.S. dollar. Since governments are tempted to create fiat money at their whim to acquire goods at no cost, some economists advocate that money should always be backed by gold or something else of real value to prevent such skullduggery. With a required backing to money, governments would then have to limit their takings to taxes and tariffs.

Even using gold as money won't bring us a free lunch. Irrespective of the form or amount of money, one's wealth is still limited to what one produces, and the prosperity of a community is limited to the sum of each member's production. If Earth were to be hit (very softly!) by a huge meteorite of pure gold, and we each received an equal share, after putting the artistic and electronic benefits of gold aside, we would not be better off. With our new-found gold as money, it might now take a kilogram (32.15 troy ounces) of gold to buy a suit, whereas pre-meteorite that same suit could have been purchased for the equivalent of one ounce. Financial wealth is measured by what one can acquire with money, not by the quantity of money itself.

13

MEANINGLESS EARNING GAPS

THE NEWS TODAY INUNDATES us with misleading statements and statistics. What does the oft-stated claim "The poor are getting poorer and the rich are getting richer" imply? Does the statement imply that the poor are becoming poorer than they were previously, while the rich are becoming richer than they were previously? If so, data will refute that notion. The state of humanity is improving as a whole, and the standard of living of each quintile[20] of wealth is also improving.[21] But this overall view doesn't provide a clear picture, either.

The U.S. Census Bureau reports that those in the highest quintile earn about 50 percent of the total income generated, while those in the lowest earn 3.5 percent. You would expect this statistic to mean that 20 percent of the people earn 50 percent of the income. Wrong! Census figures are tracked by household. There are many more working people in the top quintile than in the lowest—namely, 70 million versus 40 million. On average, the people in the highest quintile have more education, and they work one-third more hours than those in the poorest quintile,

---

[20]The ranking of five equal segments of a population from lowest (first quintile) to highest (fifth quintile).

[21]Julian Simon, *The State of Humanity* (Cambridge, Mass.: Blackwell Publishers, 1995).

many of whom are just part-time workers.[22] This is not surprising, since most people realize that obtaining an education and working more hours are advantageous to gaining wealth.

When we hear reports about the poor, who make up the lowest quintile of income, we seem to envision a fixed group of people. Yet how many of us individuals of middle-age or older are no longer in that quintile, but were at one time in our early lives part of it? Very likely, most of us. Census income figures are inherently misleading because they are based only on snapshots of a population. Income figures do not track population mobility—that is, the movement of people from one income group to another over a period of time.

We do know that those who make up the lowest income group are far younger on average than those in the upper income groups. Consider a thought experiment in which each person begins adult life in the lowest quintile of income and moves to each of the next higher quintiles as the person ages.[23] If such were the case, the income inequality between groups would be absolutely meaningless. The greater the income mobility, the less meaningful the income gaps would be. So how mobile are we relative to actual income groups?

A University of Michigan study using data from the Panel Study of Income Dynamics found that, in the U.S., only 5 percent of those in the lowest quintile in 1975 were still in that quintile by 1991. By that latter year, most (59.3 percent) had mobilized to occupy the two top quintiles (30.3 percent and 29.0 percent), while the balance (35.6 percent) mobilized to the second and third quintiles (14.6 percent and 21 percent). There was also downward mobility with over one-third of those in the top quintile in 1975

---

[22]Robert Rector and Rea Hederman, Jr., "Two Americas: One Rich, One Poor? Understanding Income Inequality in the United States, Heritage Foundation," www.Heritage.org.

[23]Glen Whitman, ECON 309, Spring 2007, Lecture #13: Economic Myths and Reality. The lecture syllabus can be found at http://www.csun.edu/~dgw61315/econ309.html.

occupying a lower quintile in 1991. During a shorter period of time (1979–1988), the U.S. Treasury reported that only 14.2 percent remained in the lowest quintile, while 39.7 percent had moved to the upper two quintiles (25.3 percent and 14.4 percent). Therefore, it's misleading to look at income shares for each quintile and say, "The rich got richer and the poor got poorer." Why? Because the people who were poor at the beginning of the time period are not (entirely) the same people who were poor at the end of the time period (and likewise for the rich).[24]

While all quintiles show gains in real earnings, it is also true that the higher quintiles show greater dollar gains than the lowest quintile—which is good news, since virtually all of us progress along the path to greater wealth.

Notwithstanding all these facts, we have yet to address the crux of what "financial inequality" means. While the statement "The poor are getting poorer and the rich are getting richer" is false, underlying this statement lingers the notion that society would be better off if there were smaller or no financial gaps between people's income. Addressing this underlying notion is of greater social and economic significance than are the facts that refute the statement stemming from the notion. The quintessential question here is: "Would society be better off without financial inequalities?"

Those who claim that the earnings gap is "worsening" imply by the very use of that word that something is bad and needs correction. John Kenneth Galbraith saw this widening gap between the rich and the poor as a moral crime. Those making this claim imply by their statements that if the rich were less rich, then the poor would be less poor. However, that is a fallacy. Such fallacies make good news fodder, of course, and are extremely useful for free rider groups to lobby for more welfare programs and higher tax rates for the rich.

Earning wealth is neither a zero-sum nor a negative-sum game. If Joe earns 1 X, and Tom earns 10 Xs, what can Joe do to

---

[24]Ibid.

get 2 Xs? Does Joe have to take an X from Tom or from someone else? Of course not. It depends on what Joe does to increase his productivity. Joe can gain 20 Xs without lowering Tom's Xs—or anyone else's. It doesn't matter if others gain more Xs. Their gain does not prevent Joe from gaining Xs too.

Joe's earnings worsen if his Xs decrease and improve if his Xs increase, regardless of the amount of Xs Tom earns. The words "worsen" and "improve" do not apply to earning gaps between different people. Such terms only apply to current earnings of individuals and entities relative to their earnings during an earlier period.

14

THE FUTILE QUEST FOR ECONOMIC EQUALITY

SOME CLAIM THAT, WHILE free markets produce an abundance of wealth, it is still inhuman and unjust that some receive more than others. They claim that free markets create great injustices by exacerbating the inequities of wealth. Furthermore, these people believe that such injustices require the intervention of those with humanitarian sentiments to reallocate wealth more equitably. While egalitarians use numerous schemes to equalize wealth, their goal is, in the end, unattainable, irrespective of their efforts. Attempts to equalize wealth will only result in reducing its quantity without affecting its allocation.

According to the Fraser Institute's *Economic Freedom of the World: 2005 Annual Report*,[25] regardless of the degree of economic freedom[26] among 128 countries (comprising 93 percent of the world's population), the percentage share of income by quintiles

---

[25]Erik Gartzke, James D. Gwartney, and Robert A. Lawson, *Economic Freedom of the World: 2005 Annual Report* (Vancouver, B.C.: Fraser Institute, 2005); www.FraserInstitute.ca.

[26]The index of economic freedom is based on the degree of personal choice, freedom of voluntary exchange, protection of person and property, the right to keep earnings, and the freedom to enter and compete in markets.

from 1998 to 2002 remained about the same in each country. According to the report, countries with greater freedom had a higher per capita income than those with less freedom. However, irrespective of the average level of per capita income of a country, the percentage distribution of such income for ascending quintiles settled at about 6 percent, 11 percent, 15 percent, 21 percent, and 47 percent.

So what do these figures tell us? It appears that income quintile tiers are a natural distribution phenomenon and remain largely unchanged (in terms of percentage), regardless of the varied attempts by governments or well-meaning politicos to equalize them. While the percentage share of each quintile is similar, irrespective of the country, the actual dollar income of each quintile increases dramatically as a country's level of freedom increases.

When the countries were grouped into quintiles based on their level of freedom (least free to most free), the average annual per capita income was about $2,000, $5,000, $6,000, $14,000, and $25,000. These figures reveal that those in the poorest quintile of the freest countries earn substantially more than those in the richest quintile of the least free countries. Those wishing to close the gap between the rich and the poor (by restricting individual liberty and transferring wealth) will not change the relative gap, but only reduce real earnings for everyone, and, in the process, harm the poorest the most. In other words, any attempt to enforce equality reduces the size of the economic pie, but not the differences in the relative slices of the pie. Regardless of the size of the pie at any given time, a fifth of the population will share in about 6 percent of that pie, while the other quintiles will each share approximately 11 percent, 15 percent, 21 percent, and 47 percent of the pie, respectively.

The gap between the earnings of the lowest and the highest quintiles at any given time is about 40 percent, but the dollar gap between them will depend on the prosperity of the country. When we hear that the gap between the lowest and highest quintiles is widening, the gap refers to dollars. Of course, if the percentage gap remains the same and the overall dollar prosperity doubles, the previous dollar gap will also double. Thus, the dollar gaps between quintiles will widen with greater prosperity, with each quintile gaining about the same percentage of the total gain. It is important to emphasize that these studies are based on snapshots of the current earnings of members of a country and do not account for income mobility. Income mobility, as discussed earlier, diminishes the significance of earning gaps, whether they are expressed in percentage or in dollar figures.

While the University of Michigan and the U.S. Treasury Department's studies demonstrate considerable mobility to higher income quintiles for people in the U.S., I'm not aware of a study that has compared the degree of mobility relative to a country's level of economic freedom. Intuitively, however, it would seem that the greater the economic freedom, the greater the degree of mobility, because greater freedom allows one to reap more of the fruit of one's own labor. This self-rewarding feature of freedom is the quintessential incentive that can lead a person to higher productivity and earnings.

15

THE ASTONISHING GREATNESS
OF INEQUALITY

WHEN FREE MARKETS CREATE wealth, regardless of how wealthy
one individual becomes, someone else, as noted above, is also better off.[27] In a market in which new technologies are emerging at
unprecedented rates, we would expect that those on the frontier
of those technologies would experience extraordinary incomes.
For some that income has been astronomic. The billionaires of
those industries have had an unbelievable impact—directly and
indirectly—on virtually everyone in the world. The benefits
they've created for the present generations and for future generations are immeasurable, but, undoubtedly, they would add up to
many times more than all the billions earned by the richest of the
rich. If we experience as many breakthroughs in the next fifty
years as we've seen in the past fifty, we can expect to see a continued increase in the number of billionaires, pushing the highest
quintile of wealth to even higher levels, while granting all of us
the benefits of those breakthroughs.

---

[27]When wealth is gained from involuntary transactions such as in takings by
a king, Mafia, or the State, someone else is worse-off.

Those in the lower quintiles will continue to increase their wealth as well, since the upper quintiles can't gain without pulling the other quintiles up with them—wealth begets wealth, as discussed earlier. Still, as the number of billionaires increases, many egalitarians will moan about "how sad that is," while in reality, the greater the number of billionaires, the better off we all will be, collectively. The wealth of billionaires represents revolutionary ideas that come from exceptional individuals who push technology, create and facilitate markets, invent ways to increase productivity, or entertain us in new ways.

Some of these superstars will create benefits for us that future generations will enjoy many centuries after their creation. Imagine what we have already gained and what our descendants will continue to gain from the talent of one exceptional man: Ludwig van Beethoven. How much would he be owed today if we were to compensate him for all the joy he has given us over time and will continue to give us in the future?[28] Imagine our lives today without the incredible creations of Alexander Graham Bell, Guglielmo Marconi, the Wright brothers, Henry Ford, Jonas Salk, or Bill Gates. These people represent those who have deeply enriched our lives and deserve our deepest gratitude.

We often hear that those who have earned great wealth should "give something back," as though they had taken something from society. Such resentful notions stem from the misconception of how wealth is earned. Contrary to such notions, those of wealth have not taken anything from society, but, in fact, have given to society an amount of wealth that far exceeds the amount they have earned.

---

[28] Additionally, the ability to enjoy Ludwig van Beethoven's work by virtually everyone is due to the sound replication technology that began with Thomas Edison's invention of the gramophone.

16

HAMPERING INEQUALITY

TRY TELLING A PROSPECTIVE lottery player, "If you win, you must share your winnings with everyone equally, including those who didn't buy tickets." Would the person buy a ticket? Obviously not.

Some view wealthy people as possessing more than their fair share, but this perception fails to acknowledge the risk that these people took against the high odds of failure. Many have taken risks by going to school and deferring income during a good part of their lives. Physicians take risks by studying and working nearly thirty years of their lives before they can begin to reap the benefits of their investment, and that's if they successfully make it to the end of that journey. Most who try don't make it! We see the Gateses, the Edisons, and the Fords, but we never hear of the countless Joneses and Smiths who tried their hand at grabbing the golden ring and simply became forgotten souls. What gratitude should we pay, even owe, to the winners who persevered through skill and hard work, took chances, and, as a result, left as their legacy a stream of goods and services that continue to better our lives?

For every Hollywood star, there are a thousand more hopefuls who have spent their lives in pursuit of stardom. Take away the glory of stardom, and we lose the thousands upon thousands who would not have staked their skills and hard work and taken a chance to become one of the stars who entertain us. Take away the glory of wealth, and we lose the millions upon millions of entrepreneurs, inventors, and pioneers who would not have staked their skills, hard work, and chances to become one of the few moguls of industry who improve our well-being. Many of those who never become stars or moguls will, nevertheless, benefit us along the way because of their efforts.

If a factory owner had only machines, with some machines that were more productive than others, wouldn't the owner take special care of his best producers? Even so, the owner wouldn't throw a wrench into *any* of them, since the output of the factory is the total of all the machines. Like machines, some people are more productive than others. Whether one's greater productivity is due to talent, skill, hard work, or simple luck, the sum of all production is the true yardstick that measures the prosperity of a society. A society's prosperity is based on the productivity of all its members, so it would be irrational to impair the productivity of those having the greater talent or skill, just as it would be irrational to throw a wrench into the more productive factory machines.

17

REDISTRIBUTION OF EARNINGS AND WEALTH

WHETHER OR NOT YOU'RE a millionaire, virtually all of your dollars are redistributed to others from the very moment they are earned. That redistribution of your money, when voluntary, can take a path of spending, lending (investing), or giving. The portion of the money that you choose not to spend will take the paths of redistribution based on someone else's choices.

The money itself provides no direct benefit to its holder until it is exchanged for something having utility. In other words, if money can't be exchanged for something that is valued, it is useless and, therefore, worthless. Whether you hold one dollar or one million dollars makes no difference in wealth; the so-called millionaire and the pauper are equally poor. Only if an individual can use those dollars in exchange for something that has utility to the person do the dollars become valuable.

Let's trace the dollars that someone actually spends. When a person builds a house, every item involved in the building of that house—concrete, wood, metal, glass—comes from raw materials that have zero value, until someone gives them utility. The metal in pipes comes from iron ore that is useless until someone digs it out of the earth, another person refines it, another machines it into pipes, another delivers it, and another installs it. This is true of every item in the house—be it wood from a tree in the forest that becomes a frame, a floor, and a roof, or be it sand from a beach that becomes glass in a window or a mirror. All these items in their raw, natural state are as useless to a pauper as to a millionaire.

The value of the raw materials in building a house is the same, irrespective of the size of a house. The only difference between a large house and a tiny one is the number of people who are compensated for infusing utility into those raw materials. In a similar vein to building a house, consider the valueless musical symbols that go into the creation of a concert. The money spent to experience the joy of music is distributed to a composer who arranges worthless, nonmaterial symbols in a unique sequence and to the musicians who give those symbols utility by producing pleasurable sounds from their instruments.

The portion of one's money that is not spent but, instead, placed in a bank account will be distributed immediately to borrowers who purchase houses and cars, and who, in turn, redistribute those dollars to those who infuse utility into otherwise useless materials. From the moment of receipt, the totality of the money that each of us has earned is thus transferred and redistributed to others—every last cent, except for the few dollars we may be carrying in our pocket or purse.

I am reminded here of one dinner guest's statement that no one should be allowed to own a yacht. Like houses, yachts are also built from useless raw materials that gain utility because of the efforts of various people, each receiving a share of the expenditure—in this case, made by wealthy yacht owners. In 1990, the U.S. government passed a luxury tax under the Omnibus Budget Reconciliation Act that applied to the sale of yachts. So what should we expect as a result of this new tax, knowing that people will act in their own self-interest? Many potential buyers either didn't buy yachts or circumvented the law by buying them from foreign makers. The lawmakers thought the tax would generate more revenue, but it backfired in two ways. It resulted in less tax being collected (from buyers, workers, and yacht builders) and caused bankruptcies of yacht companies.[29] The law was soon repealed because of the outcry, not from discontented would-be yacht buyers, but from discontented yacht builders and workers unintentionally removed from the earning redistribution path chosen by the yacht buyers.

The proposition that the State should take control of a large share of a wealthy person's earnings by taxation means that the State, instead of the earner, will determine its distribution. In this case, the distribution by the State is made, regardless of a recipient's productivity.

In short, all money is fully redistributed, whether voluntarily by the person earning it or by the State after acquiring it from the earner. Of these two methods of redistribution, which one appears fairer and more humanitarian? Which one do you believe is more peaceful and will lead to greater prosperity for more people? Which method of redistribution would you choose for the betterment of your life if you were behind John Rawls's "veil of ignorance"?[30]

---

[29]Elda DiRe, "Luxury Tax (Federal Taxation)," CPA *Journal online* (October 1991).

[30]John Rawls (1921–2002), A *Theory of Justice* (Boston: Belknap Press, 1971; rev. ed., 1999). The "veil of ignorance" is a thought experiment in which Rawls proposes that the basic structure of a just society is one whose adopted rules are arrived at by the consent (contract) of all its members, who at the time of consent and prior to the application of such rules ("*the original position*") are unaware (behind a "*veil of ignorance*") of the natural fortune or social circumstances of the person in whose body and mind they will live while adhering to the application of such rules.

18

Hiring and Firing: What Is Fair?

"It is not fair that companies can terminate their workers to increase profits" was one of the statements made at the dinner party that evening. Why employ someone in the first place? Does an employer hire to see someone work and earn a living or to reduce national unemployment figures? Of course not! Entrepreneurs create companies in pursuit of their own self-interests. And when they create these companies, they do not do so in a vacuum. First and foremost, they are dependent upon customers, their real bosses, who must be lured away from competing choices in the marketplace. Second, they must lure employees away from competing employers by offering a more profitable, or more interesting, opportunity. Once hired, these new employees must continually be pleased; otherwise they will move on to the next employer who *will* please them. Third, entrepreneurs must be able to produce their goods and services at costs that are less than the revenue received from their customers.

Since revenues will vary as market demand for products and services varies, companies must be able to vary expenses, as well. If one were prohibited from reducing the number of employees to reduce company expenses, as was suggested, one should be prohibited from reducing every other expense, too. Why? Every expense is someone else's revenue, and when expenses are cut, someone's job is jeopardized. If one stops having the windows washed to reduce expenses, then the window washer is terminated. If the employer decides not to have the annual company Christmas party, he is terminating caterers.

If an employer is prevented from terminating employees to increase profits or reduce losses, the employer will be reluctant to hire them in the first place. In essence, if you can't fire, you don't hire. So the statement made by my guest that evening ("No company should be allowed to terminate employees simply to increase profits") is proposing, in effect, that employers should not be allowed to hire employees to make a profit, either.

19

JOBS AND PROSPERITY

JOBS THEMSELVES DO NOT necessarily create prosperity; prosperity is created by the production of goods and services that people value. Make-work jobs that do not generate goods or services valued by others will not generate prosperity.

To illustrate, let's say a fire damages a house in a community. The local carpenter is not saddened, since this fire will give him an opportunity to earn a handsome sum. Of course, what the carpenter earns, the homeowner loses. "Well," you might argue, "it's a zero-sum game in terms of money, but the carpenter has a job, and it is his work on the house that is a net positive for the community."

However, the unseen part of the picture is *what* the carpenter would have been doing if he were not restoring the house. The community is no better off after restoring the house than it was before the destruction. Thus, the community has not gained prosperity.[31] If the carpenter had, instead, built a new house, the community would have increased its prosperity by gaining a new house.

---

[31]The restoration of the damaged house does improve the community from *that* point in time, but it does not improve the community from the point in time prior to the damage.

One may ask: What if the carpenter were idle at the time of the fire damage to the house? If a given vocation is filled with idle time, it means that the services being offered have a lower preference by consumers than the quantity available. In a community, vocations are chosen that provide services where consumer preferences have eliminated idle time, while the vocations experiencing idle time are avoided. This free-market feedback will lead to a higher overall prosperity of the community, because productivity will progress in the direction of greater preferences that actually reflect the subjective values of individual consumers. Therefore, if idle time were to be filled with make-work projects, the workers attracted to those projects would be diverted from otherwise productive occupations that offered services that consumers prefer.

If jobs and work are benefits for the community, we could propose burning all the houses to keep all members of the community busy working. We are, of course, struck by the absurdity of such a notion, because common sense tells us so. We envision mass displacement of people in the community who would have to divert their time and energy from their previous activities to tasks that will merely restore their community to its condition before the mass destruction. However, once the restoration begins, some might conclude that all is not bad—after all, everybody is working and earning money. As in wartime, we sense prosperity because we are all hard at work producing tanks, ships, and myriad other war-related materials, but we lose sight of the cars, yachts, and countless other useful goods that do not get produced during that same period and thus cannot be enjoyed. We lose all the unseen things that would have been produced by those soldiers and workers who are now marching, fighting, and laboring for a different purpose.

20

DIVISION OF LABOR: THE MIRACULOUS CORNUCOPIA

TODAY, SELF-SUFFICIENCY, FOR the most part, has been replaced by the division of labor. With self-sufficiency, one's consumption is limited to only that which one produces. As such, consumption is limited primarily to the essentials for survival—namely food and shelter. It is quite obvious that, in self-sufficiency, one's prosperity is simply the sum of personal production. In a division of labor, one limits one's own production to specific goods and services and depends on the production by others for the balance of what one desires to consume. The difference between a community where there is a division of labor and one where each person is self-sufficient is that with a division of labor one person's production is exchanged for that of another. Thus, regardless of the form of labor, one's production remains the determinant of one's prosperity, and the sum of each person's prosperity determines the prosperity of the entire community.

The division of labor allows each person to produce the good or service for which that person is well-suited, thereby increasing that person's own potential prosperity per unit of effort. It doesn't matter if one can produce everything better than another person, only that one can produce certain things better than one can produce other things. Bill Gates may be able to develop computer software and also mow his lawn better than his gardener, but both are better off if Gates just develops software and leaves the mowing to his gardener. Thus, enhancing each person's unique ability to increase individual prosperity enhances the prosperity of the community.

21

Is There a Limit to the Number of Jobs?

MANY PEOPLE BELIEVE THAT there is a finite number of jobs in the world, and that when one person gets one of these jobs, another must lose one. If this idea were true, our country's labor force would still be the size it was when the Pilgrims landed.

If each person were self-sufficient, consuming only that which the person produced, the idea of a finite number of jobs would make no sense. A self-sufficient farmer remains unaffected when someone else starts a farm or another form of livelihood. The difference between self-sufficiency and a division of labor is that, instead of consuming only what you produce, you exchange your products for someone else's.

In 1976, the California civilian labor force was eight million; today it is eighteen million. Where did all those jobs come from, and who lost them? Today we hear complaints about Mexican immigrants taking jobs from Americans. Legal or not, they are not reducing jobs for others. This notion is far from new. Immigrants from Mexico are just the villains of the day. In years past, it was the Irish, the Polish, the Italian, and the Chinese immigrants.[32]

---

[32]Brian Frazelle, "The Truth about Immigrants: Xenophobia Existed in Early America," *Houston Catholic Worker* 19, no. 7 (1999).

Possibly because of the small group/large group disparity and our instinctive abilities to assess economic events, immigrants who are known personally are never seen as a negative; it's only the unseen anonymous immigrants who are disliked.[33] Most accept the idea that two people can produce more benefits for each other than each person producing alone. There's no known point at which a million people stop benefiting because of the addition of one more productive person.

Labor unions use the "take away jobs" fallacy when jobs are so narrowly defined that one is allowed to do only one's job designation. A plumber isn't allowed to remove a wall to repair a pipe, because doing so would eliminate the carpenter's job. History is replete with such nonsensical restrictions.

With unionized job restrictions, inefficiency raises the cost of products and services, which, in turn, reduces consumer preference for those products and services. This "take away jobs" fallacy also caused riots, killings, and the destruction of property when labor-intensive factories installed labor-saving machines. Yet, when factories installed those machines, the demand for their now lower priced products, in most cases, resulted in an increase in the need for workers in those very same industries. Many get upset when companies take advantage of cheaper labor in poorer countries to produce goods or provide services. But what's the difference if a company in Detroit decides to send its car parts to Arkansas or somewhere out of the country for assembly? There may be a relocation of people performing a given type of job, or a change in the type of job for those who live in Detroit, but it does not reduce the number of total jobs.

When a company produces a good at a lower cost, it can, in turn, attract more buyers by reducing the price of that good to the public. The lower price of such a good frees the purchaser to use the savings to buy something additional that the purchaser could not

---

[33]Rita J. Simon, "Immigration and American Attitudes," *Public Opinion* 10, no. 2 (July/August 1987): 47–50.

have previously afforded. That "something additional" now has to be produced by someone who landed a previously nonexistent job.

Some are intrigued by the recent "wonders" of the European work ethic: apparently everyone enjoys more leisure time, with less time devoted to work. Europeans have mandated shorter workweeks—approximately six vacation weeks per year, and numerous holidays. Supposedly, this scheduling creates more jobs and greater prosperity; as long as everyone has a job, the economy thrives, irrespective of what or how much one produces. But can this concept be correct? Of course not! When people don't work, products don't get produced, and when products don't get produced, prosperity can't be realized.

Furthermore, tenure policies adopted by some governments to protect jobs (so employees can't be fired) engender mediocre work, companies' reluctance to hire, and an inability to compete in world markets. In France, the average workweek (including vacations) is about twenty-seven hours; in the U.S., the average is thirty-five hours.

Fewer work hours do not create more jobs and prosperity, as was theorized by the French in an attempt to alleviate their nagging high unemployment rate. To illustrate, assume a job (a task of producing a good) can be accomplished by one person in an eight-hour day. If the law prohibits a person from working more than one hour per day, then eight persons would be required to complete the same job. Even though eight persons are now employed, the task is still a single, eight-hour job. Such a law does nothing but dilute the prosperity created by spreading the production of one job among eight people. Now, instead of seven people being unemployed for eight hours a day, we simply have eight people unemployed for seven hours a day.

Enforcing shorter workweeks to increase jobs and prosperity is not a new concept. Economists John Maynard Keynes (1883–1946) and John Kenneth Galbraith (1908–2006) proposed such nonsense decades ago. Imagine if you were a self-sufficient farmer and were told by your political leader that you must spend less time plowing, seeding, and harvesting in order to have more to eat. You would most likely want to commit that poor soul to an asylum.

Shorter workweeks and rigid tenure legislation only reduce people's productive potential. It is productivity that improves living conditions, and those States that adopt rigid labor laws will find themselves falling behind those States with more flexible labor laws. But the individuals who circumvent these policies counter some of the negative effects of rigid labor laws. When the State restricts one's ability to hire and another's ability to work, the human spirit will create arrangements that will bring them together in myriad ingenuous ways that no law or enforcement can totally prevent. The ratio of work time to leisure time is a personal preference, and when the State dictates the ratio, those who think otherwise will find ways to get the final word.

Of course it is not only rigid labor laws that entice individuals to circumvent those laws. Any law that restricts the production of goods and services has a similar enticement for individuals to circumvent that law, as well. Fortunately for these productive individuals, we have free underground markets that make available goods and services that would otherwise not exist. Italy is a great example of a country with such markets. Its underground economy is estimated at between 15 percent and 25 percent of the Gross National Product (GNP) and tax evasion is a national pastime. The underground economy of Europe is estimated at between 7 percent and 16 percent of GNP.[34] If everyone were to obey the laws to their full intent, many countries would be far less prosperous than they are currently.

This is true in the U.S. as well. Despite hundreds of thousands of restrictive regulations, many find ways to offer goods and services that are prohibited by law. Violators risk being caught and fined or incarcerated; however, the sheer abundance of the regulations, coupled with the abundance of violators, reduces the likelihood of any one of them being caught.

---

[34]National Center for Policy Analysis. http://www.ncpa.org/ba/ba278.html, Brief Analysis, no. 278 (1998).

22

FEAST AND FAMINE

SOME BELIEVE THERE IS a static quantity of resources in the world and that whatever one person consumes leaves that much less for someone else. It is true that at any given time there is a finite supply of available resources; however, as supplies are consumed, they are replenished or replaced with substitutes.

Let's look at one of the most important resources—food. From 1964 to 1999, world food consumption per day in kilocalories per capita increased from 2,358 to 2,803 (19 percent). During this same period, developing countries experienced an increase from 2,054 to 2,681 (31 percent) kilocalories.[35] With 22 percent fewer acres and 74 percent fewer farm workers, U.S. farmers are able to produce enough food to feed twice the number of Americans and export eight times the amount of food than they did in 1950.[36] In 1950, it took an American an average of one-and-a-half hours of labor to earn one loaf of bread, one-half gallon of

[35]World Health Organization, technical report series 916, "Diet, Nutrition and the Prevention of Chronic Diseases," chap. 3; http://www.fao.org/docrep/005/AC911E/ac911e05.htm#bm05.

[36]Milton Hallberg, "U.S. Farm Policy: Are New Approaches Needed?" *Farm Economics* 4 (2001).

milk and three pounds of chicken; by 1997, it took only twenty-five minutes to do the same.[37]

While famine still exists in some parts of the world, the feasting by people in other parts is not the cause. If all the food being produced in the world today were evenly divided among all inhabitants, there would be sufficient supplies to eliminate all hunger.[38] However, because of the tragedy of the commons, if all the food were to be evenly divided, the amount of food produced would fall to levels where all would go hungry.

Virtually everyone can be sufficiently productive to earn the necessities of life. Imagine if there were no borders or State restrictions on where one was allowed to move, live, work, or conduct business. People in need of food would migrate to places in need of their services, and companies in need of workers would move to or emerge where people need food.

Without the dictates of a ruler (State or otherwise), how long, in a free economy, would it take to see famine, for the most part, disappear? In today's world, famine is caused by political policies that restrict free human interaction. Foreign aid is not the solution; it has had no positive impact (and possibly even a negative impact) on the so-called "poverty trap."[39]

Some believe that if there were fewer people in the world, everyone would have more to consume and be more prosperous. We hear that people in Africa and Mexico would not be so poor if they had fewer children. The Malthusian fear of population growth, although fallacious, is widely believed and acted upon by

---

[37]W. Michael Cox and Richard Alm, *Myths of Rich and Poor: Why We're Better Off Than We Think* (New York: Basic Books 1999), p. 43.

[38]"Global Food Trends: Prospects for Future Food Security," http://www.unsystem.org/scn/archives/scnnews11/ch14.htm.

[39]James D. Gwartney, Robert A. Lawson, and William Easterly, *Economic Freedom of the World: 2006 Annual Report*, chap. 2: Freedom Versus Collectivism in Foreign Aid," The Fraser Institute (www.fraserinstitute.ca).

many governments.[40] In Julian Simon's *Population Matters*, the chapter "Why Do We Still Think Babies Cause Poverty?" points to a dozen studies that show "that faster population growth is not associated with slower economic growth."[41]

Population density doesn't cause poverty, either. If that were so, Japan, New York City, and Hong Kong would be some of the poorest areas of the world. It isn't abundant natural resources that create prosperity either, since none of these areas ranks high on that list. The idea that fewer people equates to greater prosperity is put to rest by Julian Simon in *Population Matters*, in which the author questions why our ancestors weren't more prosperous when there were just a few thousand of us on the planet. During the past two hundred years, world population has increased six-fold, but the world output has increased eighty-fold.[42]

One of the points I've emphasized in this book is that, given time, human ingenuity will always outmaneuver bureaucrats and circumvent State prohibitions when those prohibitions stand in the way of individual prosperity. An exemplary case of such human ingenuity takes place every day along the border between the United States and Mexico. Despite heavy border patrols, immigration restrictions, and a major language barrier, many millions of Mexicans have found their way to those who want their services. An underground network of facilitators has evolved to help merge the complementary needs of Americans and Mexicans.

Some argue that we must limit the number of immigrant workers entering the U.S. because we can't assimilate them all.

---

[40]"The Principle of Population" by Thomas Robert Malthus (1766–1834) was based on the idea that population, if unchecked, increases at a geometric rate (e.g., 1, 2, 4, 8, 16, etc.), whereas the food supply grows at an arithmetic rate (e.g., 1, 2, 3, 4, 5, etc.).

[41]Julian Simon, *Population Matters: People, Resources, Environment, and Immigration* (New Brunswick, N.J.: Transaction Publishers, 1990).

[42]David Osterfeld, "Overpopulation: The Perennial Myth," *The Freeman* (September 1993).

The very reason they keep coming is proof that they can be assimilated. If no one wanted to hire them, they would simply stop coming. There is no need for a central planner to determine how many immigrant workers we can assimilate; the marketplace will determine that number with utmost efficiency.

The major hindrances to bringing employers and Mexican workers together are Mexico's laws that regulate, prohibit, and restrict the operations of foreign-owned businesses. If foreign companies were free to make the most of Mexican labor without such restrictions, it would not be necessary for so many workers to leave their families to find work here—employers would accommodate them where they live. If Mexico's political rulers (not to be excluded from other rulers) wanted to improve the living conditions of Mexicans, they could simply lift the restrictions on foreign ownership, drastically reduce taxes, and eliminate regulations relative to labor, imports, and exports. Then they could sit back and let the market bring prosperity to their country. It does not require any planning; prosperity evolves spontaneously. Beyond the opposition to such plans by rulers are those concerned that foreign entrepreneurs will exploit cheap labor in poor countries and get rich in the process. But the very possibility of getting rich is what will bring those with that dream to those who want a better life and are eager to find a way out of poverty.

23

THEFT AND PROSPERITY

ONE'S GOODS CAN BE transferred to another person voluntarily, as in trade, or involuntarily, as in theft. In a voluntary transfer of goods, both parties gain because each party values the goods received more than the goods relinquished. However, more essential than the value gained in a trade is the prerequisite that each party must have produced something of value in order to carry out the trade.

One's labor (a service) is no different. Labor can be provided voluntarily, as in a job, or involuntarily, as in slavery. One's willingness to provide an hour of work in exchange for X dollars means that a worker values X dollars more than the hour of his labor, while the employer or client values that hour of service more than X dollars. The prosperity of a voluntary society is the sum of each person's production of goods and services, plus the added value realized as those goods and services are traded in the marketplace.

In an involuntary transfer of goods, such as theft, one party suffers a loss while another party realizes a gain. In such cases, the prosperity of a society is only enhanced by the victim's production of goods; the thief, as a member of that same society, does not enhance its prosperity. With theft, society does not realize the thief's potential productivity. Additionally, society continues to lose as long as the threat of theft exists. That threat hinders a producer's incentive to produce; it also diminishes his production because some of his time and energy is diverted from productive activity to defensive activity.

Taxation has a similar effect on the productivity of the members of a society. With taxation, a society's prosperity is diminished by all the benefits that could otherwise have been realized from the productivity of those involved in enforcing and collecting taxes. The productivity is further diminished by all that could otherwise be realized from those acting as professional tax consultants, and further still by the disincentive to produce and by the amount of the taxpayer's productive energy that is diverted to defensive activity, and even further by the production that might have been realized by otherwise productive members of society who are being subsidized with a portion of the tax.

To illustrate, let's return to our five-person community, in which each member is producing 20 units of goods per time period. What happens if one member—let's call him Fred—stops producing, and, instead, decides to take 20 percent (four units) of each of the others' production? At first, it appears the group's production is reduced from 100 units to 80 units, with each member, including Fred, equally enjoying 16 units of wealth. However, the loss of Fred's production is not the only loss to the community. Additionally, each of the four producing members must now expend some of their time and energy trying to defend against Fred's intrusion. Their time defending takes away from their time producing, resulting in fewer units being produced. Now, instead of producing 20 units each, they only have the time and energy to produce 15. As a result, the community's prosperity has decreased to 60 units, with each member, including Fred, only enjoying 12 units.

Unfortunately, this is not the end of the damage caused by Fred. He discovers that, by giving some of his takings to certain members of the community, he can gain enough support to thwart a revolt and increase the level of future takings. To illustrate, let's say Fred, in our five-person community, decides to share some of his takings by offering to subsidize the lowest producing members of that society (besides himself).

Before Fred's "gracious" offer, each of the four productive members was producing 15 units of prosperity and enjoying only 12 units, since 3 of their units were going to Fred. Now, let's say one member is more industrious and produces more than the others. Fred, keeping his promise, gives one of "his" units to each of the other three members. By sharing his takings with lesser producers, Fred encourages some members to become slackers, while gaining their support to continue his takings from the more productive members of the community. Consequently, Fred's offer reduces the prosperity of the community even more. If Fred had simply destroyed or consumed all of his takings, the community would have been better off than by his sharing them with other members of the community. In summary, Fred has not only reduced the productivity of those from whom he has taken, but also has further reduced the productivity of those to whom he has given.

The State, like Fred, would also do less damage by not using its takings to subsidize its members. Subsidies reduce the free-market efficiencies of competition and incentives, while diverting the efforts of some from producing goods and services that people value more to those they value less or not at all. Providing subsidies to farmers to curtail production and to shirkers unwilling to work defies common sense. I recall my father telling me sometime in the 1930s about the government's policy of paying farmers to destroy their pigs.[43] Although he highly admired President Franklin Roosevelt, he could not make sense of that policy, and even though I was only a tyke at the time, it seemed rather strange to me too.

---

[43]Chris Edwards, "The Government and the Great Depression," *Cato Institute Tax and Budget Bulletin,* no. 25 (2005). Under the Agricultural Adjustment Act of 1933, while millions of Americans were going hungry, the government plowed under ten million acres of crops, slaughtered six million pigs, and left fruit to rot.

24

Intrusion by
Any Other Name

THE PROPOSITION THAT EXECUTIVES earn far too much (as was stated that evening at my dinner) reflects a fundamental philosophical view that people should not be allowed to determine the conditions of their own personal relationships. Although this proposition was aimed at prohibiting certain arrangements between associates relative to their working relationship, it is, in principle, no different from prohibiting certain arrangements between partners relative to their sexual relationship.

Either the people in a relationship have the authority to establish the conditions of their relationship (liberty) or someone outside the relationship has the authority to establish those conditions (mastery). In principle, all relationships between contracting, consenting people are personal, irrespective of the nature of those arrangements. It is inconsistent to abhor intrusion into relationships taking place in the bedroom, while embracing intrusion into relationships taking place in the boardroom, or vice versa.

While all political camps advocate intrusion into the personal affairs of individuals, the camps differ in their selection of where intrusion is proper and where it is not. Political camps are adept at morally justifying their selection of intrusions while condemning those selected by their opponents. Laws that intrude into the personal affairs and contractual arrangements between people include those that regulate the conditions of marriage (same-sex, multiple partners, interracial), conditions of employment (wages, hours, benefits), and conditions of commerce (prices, quality, products, services).

We may find the personal relationships between some people to be quite strange and possibly repulsive, and view certain employment arrangements between some people to be deplorable. We may even be appalled at the arrangements people make to exchange their goods and services. However, beyond our displeasure when considering the personal affairs of others, we should ask ourselves: "To whom do these affairs belong—them or me?" Once we forcibly intrude into the way others choose to live their lives, we open our doors to intrusion from those who don't particularly approve of the way we choose to live ours. Therefore, it behooves us to stay out of the personal affairs of others, lest we unintentionally invite them to intrude into our own personal affairs.

25

Do We Deserve
Our Good Fortune?

In 1971, *A Theory of Justice*, by John Rawls, became an immediate bestseller, with more than four-hundred-thousand copies sold—a phenomenal feat for a book dealing with economics, morality, and philosophy. As a result of this book and his other writings, Rawls, an egalitarian, is considered to be the most influential moral theorist of the twentieth century. While his writings have garnered much criticism, especially among libertarians, many agree that he rekindled what had become a fading interest in political and moral philosophy.

In *A Theory of Justice*, Rawls claims that one does not deserve the fruit of one's own innate talent. He contends that those born into the world with natural advantages over others do not deserve the financial benefits resulting from those advantages because those advantages are "accidents of natural endowment." But what he seems to miss is causality: If you threaten to take away the fruit, someone's innate talent and skill will not bother to blossom. Besides, if one does not deserve the fruit of his own talent, it hardly follows that someone else deserves it.

If Michael Jordan does not deserve the wealth that comes from his innate talent, size, and athleticism, what can be said about all the fans who have gained wealth (well-being) as a result of being able to watch him play basketball? Rawls neglects a key economic principle that when one person earns wealth, another must gain wealth. Jordan did not become wealthy by playing basketball; he became wealthy by giving millions of people the pleasure and benefit of watching him play basketball. When one buys a ticket for admission to a game or the theater, one perceives the pleasure gained from the experience to be greater than the cost of the ticket. No matter how lucky one may be in earning millions, those earnings require the granting of benefits to others of an amount greater than the dollars received by the so-called "lucky" one.

Whether one simply stumbles upon a cure for cancer or labors an entire lifetime to find it, the beneficiaries are no less the fortunate recipients of the utility of that discovery. Denigrating someone's deservedness based on good fortune is a pointless and childish enterprise. Rawls misguides us with his "difference principle,"[44] inequality is neither justified nor unjustified—it is simply natural and not subject to justification. As discussed earlier, those with special talents and skills are society's most valuable assets. Such inequalities are to be treasured, not disparaged. Any political policy aimed at justifying inequalities between the lesser advantaged and the greater advantaged would do injustice to both groups, but particularly to those who are the lesser advantaged.

Those seeking the greatest sustainable financial benefits for the least well-off group can only achieve their goal by allowing free markets to naturally bring all human beings to greater levels of well-being. By the nature of that process, those who are the least well-off will gain from those who are better off. This process will also grant the least well-off the most favorable opportunity to attain the wealth represented by those who are most well-off.

---

[44]Rawls argues that self-interested rational persons behind the "veil of ignorance" would choose two general principles of justice to structure society in the real world: (1) *Principle of Equal Liberty*: Each person has an equal right to the most extensive liberties compatible with similar liberties for all. (2) *Difference Principle*: Social and economic inequalities should be arranged so that they are both (a) to the greatest benefit of the least advantaged persons, and (b) attached to offices and positions open to all under conditions of equality of opportunity.

26

INHERITANCE

"NO ONE SHOULD BE allowed to inherit wealth," was another idea proposed at my dinner.

An essential part of the incentive to acquire assets is the underlying sense that the holder of those assets has the ability to control their disbursement; otherwise earnings would be meaningless. As mentioned earlier, one's earnings can be voluntarily spent (transferred to another), invested (lent to another), or bequeathed (given to another). When the State interferes with one's desire to bequeath those assets, one will find ways to circumvent or limit the impact of such interference. Numerous complex trusts and other vehicles have been created to circumvent inheritance interference. Undoubtedly, knowing human nature, people use many illegal maneuvers as well to accomplish similar results.

Although a death tax rate of approximately 50 percent is imposed on estates above a specified amount, very little of that tax is collected, because creative legal schemes are employed to reduce the impact. According to the IRS, estate taxes represent only about 1.25 percent of the tax revenue collected. Plug the loopholes, and new ones will soon emerge—that's the nature of human ingenuity when it is hard at work defending life and property. If it were forbidden to give assets to one's heirs, as was proposed, it would be naïve to think that such assets would, *ipso facto*, end up in the hands of the State.

When the State acquires the assets of an estate, they are simply distributed to persons other than those chosen by the earner. When one argues that heirs don't deserve the assets because they didn't earn them, what can be said about those persons who receive those assets via the State?

The individual who earned the wealth will spend, invest, and distribute his assets more discriminatingly than the State would, because the earner has a greater vested interest in the use of those assets. That vested interest may include concerns that gifting can do more harm than good. Gifting to heirs can, indeed, make their lives less rewarding and can trigger family squabbles. However, the market has, and will continue to develop, trusts and programs to help reduce a grantor's concern about the risks and potential harm that can result from the distribution of an estate. Of course, a grantor can simply bequeath a portion, or all, of the estate to nonfamily members—a common practice.

Those who support a high estate or death tax sometimes argue that a concentration of wealth can lead to an abuse of power by a wealthy family. A family would abuse power, in this case, by seizing people's property, plundering their earnings, and by waging war against competing families. *Those* are abuses of power! People who may be concerned about a *potential* abuse of power by a wealthy family should be even more gravely concerned about the *actual* abuse of power by the State at levels no family would be able to attain.

27

Using Violence to Thwart Peaceful Activity

The urge to save humanity is almost always a false front for the urge to rule.

-H.L. Mencken (1880–1956)

ANY POLITICAL PROPOSAL THAT prevents peaceful activity, in effect, condones acts of violence—coercion, incarceration, or death—upon persons who are minding their own business or interacting with other persons on a volitional and contractual basis. Peaceful activities and associations are thus condemned, because someone who is not a participant in those activities finds those activities and associations objectionable.

The proposals made that evening at my dinner party were offered not to defend against barbarians banging at the gate, but instead to control human subjects merely interacting with each other peacefully and minding their own business. To wit: One can point to the discussed peaceful interactions between the yacht builder and the yachtsman, the employer and employee, and the benefactor and the beneficiary.

A proponent of any State policy concurrently must condone the acts necessary to enforce its compliance, and by so doing, is, to some extent, responsible for the ultimate consequences of such acts. One can ascribe admirable titles to a policy and heartwarming goals to its purpose, but, regardless of the rhetoric, any act used to enforce compliance remains inconsistent with human liberty, since that compliance involves a master and a subject. It is inconsistent to despise slavery on the one hand, while condoning mastery on the other.

28

KARL MARX

WHAT EXACTLY LED TO THE collapse of the Soviet Empire? Was it communism or totalitarianism? Is there, in fact, a difference between the two?

Marx would not have condoned the tyranny used by those who acted in his name, but for Marx to expect that his words "from each according to his ability and to each according to his needs" would not be used to justify despotic acts is quite naïve for someone who called himself a scientist. Marx was not, in fact, a scientist; he saw, but ignored, the abundant data available in England that refuted his contentions.

According to Marx, all the value of a good derives from the labor that goes into its production. This *labor theory of value* is in opposition to the *subjective theory of value*, which posits the value of a good or service is determined by individuals, regardless of the time and energy (labor) that went into its production. The labor theory of value is fallacious; if it were not so, one of my paintings (God forbid!) would be as valuable as one by Vincent van Gogh.

Based on the labor theory of value, Marx claimed that workers do not get all of the proceeds from a sale because they are exploited by the rich factory owner. He further claimed that factory owners and landowners, having control of the political system, are able to siphon off a portion of the wealth in the form of profits that should, instead, flow to the workers. On this point,

Marx was wrong, even during his time and based on the conditions where he lived. Workers in London were continually improving their conditions. While surrounded by clear evidence to the contrary, he nevertheless wrote:

> In proportion as capital accumulates, the lot of the labourer, be his payment high or low, must grow worse. Accumulation of wealth at one pole is at the same time accumulation of misery, agony of toil, slavery, ignorance, brutality, mental degradation at the opposite pole.[45]

Marx's critique of capitalism is not valid, but that invalidity in and of itself is no crime. Many who read and believed his contentions indoctrinated the masses with his teachings, and that in itself is not a crime, either. But when that indoctrination failed to improve conditions as Marx had contended it would, the leaders of the movement then resorted to physical force. They tortured and killed millions by decree and starved millions of others by compulsory collectivist programs. Those actions are crimes—indeed, acts of genocide. Marx might have been appalled to see what happened, or he may have simply turned his head and ignored the evidence, as he did when he wrote his critique of capitalism.

Marx dreamed of a world where labor was a fulfillment of one's need to work, as love is a fulfillment of one's need for sex. He envisioned a world without money, private property, or inequality, in which everyone would have the greatest fulfillment of life and liberty. Although he ridiculed religion as an "opiate of the masses," his promises were, ironically, even more seductive and addictive than religion; they promised paradise here on earth. What a wonderful promise to hear when you're a struggling worker: have faith, and a Garden of Eden awaits you just around the corner.

The strategies employed by the disciples of Marx to indoctrinate the masses also resemble those used by the disciples of Christ. They each employed rituals, repetitive readings, rote declarations, strict allegiance, and a vigorous, proselytizing campaign.

---

[45]Karl Marx, *Das Kapital* (1867).

Historically and ironically, many who failed to "see" the merits of communism or failed to conform to the dogma of the church were tortured and killed. Such atrocities took the form of crusades,[46] witch hunts,[47] labor camps, forced famines, and executions of any detractors who were deemed to be traitors, sinners, heretics, or merely obstructionists.[48]

The suffering and killing of those unwilling to conform to someone else's political or religious beliefs continue in many parts of the world today. Even in this country, religious fanatics impose their dogma and values upon others by using the strong arm of the State. In this respect, although their beliefs may be at odds with those of Marxists, these believers also endorse the concept of mastery over the lives of others.

Communism, like religion, can be practiced without everyone's indulgence. I wonder whether, if Marx were alive today, he would believe as he did then. Maybe he would not scorn capitalism, but rather, accept its technologically advanced society. Those who see communism as a better way of life can now choose to live that life without the need for others to do likewise. No longer is there a need for a revolution.

Today, because of technology, one can earn the basic necessities of life in a small fraction of the time it took during the nineteenth

---

[46]Matthew White, "Selected Death Tolls for Wars, Massacres and Atrocities Before the 20th Century," http://users.erols.com/mwhite28/ warstat0.htm.

[47]Brian Levack, *The Witch-Hunt in Early Modern Europe*, 2nd ed. (London: Longman, 1995). The author estimates there were about sixty-thousand accused witches executed in Europe. The estimate of deaths by others ranges between twenty thousand and one hundred thousand from 1400 to 1800.

[48]Robert Conquest, *The Great Terror: Stalin's Purge of the Thirties* (New York: Macmillan, 1968). The author estimates those killed under Stalin by executions from 1936 to 1938 were about one million; from 1936 to 1950 about twelve million died in the camps; and three-and-a-half million died in the 1930–1936 collectivization. Overall, he concludes Stalin was responsible for at least twenty million deaths. Mao Tse-tung, another disciple of Marx, caused the death of an additional thirty million in China between 1958 and 1962.

century, when Marx lived.[49] If work, as Marx suggests, is a fulfillment of a human need (as I agree it is), one can now more easily choose a form of work that brings a personal fulfillment of that need. Fellow Marxists can form personal communes and avoid money, private property, and inequality. They can live the life that Marx dreamed of living. In a free society, they can practice their communal convictions to their heart's content—even encouraging others to join them. Such associations would not be too unlike those seen in a monastery or convent, where the lifestyles chosen by their members are voluntary. In this respect, communism is not in conflict with liberty, since the communal association with others is not one of coercion.

However, when Marxists *demand* that everyone must live their lives in the same way as Marxists do, their alleged ideology, lifestyle, and fulfillment of a need just become façades to cover up a ruthless quest for social and political power.

Despite my criticism of Marx's so-called science, his utopian promises, his fallacious labor theory of value, and his denial of the labor conditions around him, there is little doubt that Marx wanted the best for humanity. He spent his life living as he believed, and I find him to have been a man of spirit who lived by his convictions. This is also true, however, of many do-gooders who try to reform the world. They see conditions of the world that they despise and try to improve them, while, unfortunately, neither possessing nor seeking a clear understanding of causality and human nature.

Armed with misconceptions of the real world and fallacious reasoning, these reformers pound the pavement for their cause, and when they discover that their solution only worsens matters, they simply pound harder. Marx was the world's most notorious do-gooder, and those who take him to heart still keep pounding harder. Today many who despise the real world continue to find comfort in their faith in a Marxist utopian world.

---

[49]The gross domestic product (adjusted for inflation and deflation) of the material standard of living in the United States from 1820 to 1998 increased approximately twenty-two-fold, or an average of 1.73 percent per year. EH.Net Encyclopedia.

29

THE HAZARD OF EQUALIZING CONSEQUENCES

THE REGULARITIES OBSERVED IN nature guide our judgments. We infer from experience that there are causal relationships from which we can presuppose an outcome to be pursued or avoided by our actions.[50] We learn that actions and inactions have consequences, and we also favor certain consequences to others. Good judgments thus result in favorable consequences, while poor judgments result in unfavorable ones.

When the State makes one person responsible for another's poor judgment, it encourages haphazard judgments, since critical consideration of one's own actions becomes less consequential to the individual. Without the State equalizing consequences, people take greater care in the judgments they make regarding their acts and the perceived consequences of those acts. Self-reliance is a better tool than State-reliance, because it promotes prudence. Individual liberty does not guarantee better judgment, but it does gravitate in that direction via natural feedback, which benefits us

---

[50]Hans-Hermann Hoppe, *Economic Science and the Austrian Method* (Auburn, Ala.: Ludwig von Mises Institute, 1995).

when we make "right" decisions and penalizes us when we make "wrong" ones.

When people are responsible for their own actions, they have a vested interest in making "right" decisions, since they bear the primary cost of their mistakes. The saying "we learn from our mistakes" exemplifies this feedback mechanism that we intuitively use as our own personal guide through life. When the State diminishes the effect of the feedback of our mistakes, it also weakens the lessons we will learn from those mistakes.

30

SPONTANEOUS ORDER VS. INTELLIGENT DESIGN

Yet this government never of itself furthered any enterprise, but by the alacrity with which it got out of its way.
-Henry David Thoreau (1817–1862)

Good order results spontaneously when things are let alone.
-Chuang-tzu (369–286 B.C.)

SOME BELIEVE THAT THE ideal social order can be achieved only by an intelligent designer, while those who disagree contend that a social order evolves spontaneously from those forces of nature that act behind the scene and that conscious effort cannot design. The existence of complex living organisms, economic markets, and language are examples of spontaneous order that no designer could have achieved or imagined. Charles Darwin in *The Origin of Species* used the term "natural selection" to express the guiding force behind the development of increasingly more complex organisms. Adam Smith in *The Wealth of Nations* used "the invisible hand" as a similar metaphor to express the guiding force behind the increased wealth that occurs in a society wherein people act in their own self-interest.

Nature's regularities appear to follow certain laws of causality that reward or punish each of us following the actions we take. This natural feedback is the "invisible hand" from which complex living structures and highly productive markets evolve.[51] Regardless of the intended goals of social engineers, society will take its course based on the laws of causality that govern the effects of each of our actions. The unrelenting negative feedback we have witnessed following every major scheme engineered by central planners is a warning, that, if unheeded, we can reasonably expect to see the same negative feedback following similar schemes in the future.

Noted evolutionary psychologists Leda Cosmides and John Tooby describe succinctly the reason why social welfare is harmed by replacing individual decision making with decision making by a central planner:

> Significantly, the human mind was intensely selected to evolve mechanisms to evaluate its own welfare, and is so equipped by natural selection to compute and represent its own array of preferences in exquisite and often inarticulable detail. The array of n-dimensional rankings that inhabits our motivational systems is too rich to be communicated to others or represented by them, which is one reason displacing value guided decision making to remote institutions systematically damages social welfare. Under a system of private exchange, this richness need not be communicated or understood by anyone else—its power is harnessed effectively by a simple choice rule built into the human mind: pick the alternative with the highest payoff.[52]

---

[51]An exhaustive explanation of how a natural feedback system can create biological complexity is made by Richard Dawkins in his masterpiece, *The Blind Watchmaker: Why the Evidence of Evolution Reveals a Universe Without Design* (New York: W.W. Norton, 1986).

[52]Leda Cosmides and John Tooby, "Evolutionary Psychology, Moral Heuristics, and the Law," in *Heuristics and the Law*, Gerd Gigerenzer and Christoph Engel, eds. Dahlem Workshop Report 94 (Cambridge, Mass.: MIT Press, 2006).

Every day, six billion human brains are processing information about their outside world, each triggering thousands of emotions and feelings. Through these emotions and feelings we engage the world, make decisions, and act. Emotions are unique to each of us, and while they may be expressed or described, the actual emotional experience cannot be transferred to another. Groups, countries, and companies do not experience emotions, nor can they make decisions—only individuals are capable of that process.[53]

---

[53]Methodological individualism is a philosophical method aimed at explaining and understanding broad society-wide developments as the aggregation of decisions by individuals. See Ludwig von Mises, *Human Action* (Auburn, Ala.: Ludwig von Mises Institute, 1998), chap. 2: "The Principle of Methodological Individualism," sect. 4.

31

THE DISASTROUS LESSONS OF SOCIAL ENGINEERING

THOSE WHO TRY TO engineer society in a direction contrary to human nature will only become frustrated in their attempts. Forty years and $5 trillion later, the U.S. government's "War on Poverty" (à la President Lyndon Johnson, 1964) has not only failed, but also has left more poverty in its wake and ruined more families than if the government had simply done nothing.[54] In his 1984 book, *Losing Ground*, Charles Murray recounts the tragic consequences that followed the adoption of governmental social policies between 1950 and 1980, and explains why such consequences are predictable wherever welfare entitlement programs are instituted.

The government's "War on Drugs" (à la President Richard Nixon, 1969) is another example in which social engineering created a lucrative underground economy that fostered more crime and havoc than if the "war" had never begun. The government spends more than $5 billion per month (only the up-front costs) and arrests a drug violator every twenty seconds, on average,

---

[54]Michael Janofsky, *The New York Times*, 9 February 1998.

resulting in more than five-hundred-thousand arrests during the first four months of 2006.

The War on Drugs has failed abysmally to decrease drug use. Since the beginning of the "war," the use of illegal drugs has increased in all categories. The "war" was, however, successful in reducing the amount of marijuana being illegally imported into the U.S. As an unintended consequence, drug smugglers turned to cocaine, which was easier to move and gave a much higher profit margin for the weight and volume of their product. It also gave incentive to U.S. marijuana growers, who moved to meet the demand by increasing domestic marijuana production and improving its quality. The disastrous results following the government's prohibition of alcohol manufacturing, shipping, and sales from 1920 to 1933 should have served as a warning of what to expect when simply substituting the prohibition's target substance.

The forces of nature that govern health care are no different from those forces that govern other markets. With government engineering our health care, we are well on the way to another catastrophe. Government's intrusion into health care markets has been pervasive for many years. Today's escalating health care costs stem from subsidized services and the accumulation of government intervention into nearly every phase of this industry. In a free market, health care, like other goods and services, would be available at a fraction of today's costs. Consider the computer industry, in which government intervention is minuscule compared to its interference in the health care industry. In the computer industry the complexities are on a par with those of health care, yet we are constantly amazed at the dwindling prices (even with inflated dollars) for mind-boggling increases in performance. Today, virtually everyone can own a computer that just a generation ago only major corporations could have afforded.

Taking government out of the health care business is not likely for some time, but taking oneself out of the government's health care system is a choice that many patients and health care providers are making. The claim that government must get into the business of providing health care because many people can't afford it totally misses the point. Many people can't afford health care *because* government has gotten into that business. Tommy Thompson, the former Secretary of Health and Human Services, predicts that the annual costs of health care will double today's $2 trillion by 2013.[55]

The lesson from State-engineered health care, like previous lessons of resulting disasters, will most likely be misunderstood by social planners, because they will not accept nature's way of telling us that such involuntary means to improve welfare will fail to meet the intended goal, regardless of how it is engineered.

But the saddest of all failures today in the U.S. is State-engineered education, in which the very ideas of social engineering and State eminence are incorporated into the curricula.[56] Any student who can reason well will be confused between what is proper and improper conduct when they are taught that government people are authorized to act in ways that would be a crime if done by others.

Furthermore, these students will question the moral imperatives that their parents try to instill in them as a guide to a responsible and rewarding life when they see such imperatives violated by those who are revered as heroes in their history books. Aside from these moral conflicts, consider the difficulty in teaching students the benefits of freedom and the free enterprise system—historically known as the "American way." How can students appreciate the merits of free enterprise when even their schools don't operate under that system? And while making school attendance compulsory, it cannot then teach liberty and the detrimental

---

[55]"Tommy Thompson: America's Health Care System will Collapse by 2013," May 16, 2006, by Wayne Hanson. http://www.govtech.com/gt/articles/99517.

[56]California 2nd District Court of Appeals, in a decision that makes home schooling by noncertified teachers illegal, stated that a "primary purpose of the educational system is to train schoolchildren in good citizenship, patriotism, and loyalty to the state and nation as a means of protecting the public welfare." Case filed February 28, 2008. http://www.courtinfo.ca.gov/opinions/documents/B192878.PDF.

effects of coercion. The benefits of freedom and morality are not difficult matters to teach and to understand, but such teachings are virtually impossible in a State school.

Like other government-provided services, education is predictably poor in quality and high in cost. Making matters worse for U.S. public schools is the National Education Association (NEA), the largest labor union in the country, representing 3.2 million public school teachers and support personnel, and the Federation of Teachers, which is an affiliate of the AFL/CIO with one million members. The combination of unions making the termination of incompetent teachers almost impossible[57] and the difficulty parents face when attempting to transfer their child to a better performing public school accelerates the decline of a failing system. U.S. public schools fall far behind European state schools where parents have the option of choosing which school their child attends. Such choice by parents, although certainly not a free market, does at least provide some competition between State supported schools.

"At age 10, American students take an international test and score well above the international average. But by age 15, when students from 40 countries are tested, the Americans place 25th."[58] In 1998, 20,760 K–12 home-schooled students in 11,930 families were administered either the Iowa Tests of Basic Skills or the Tests of Achievement and Proficiency. The achievement test scores of this group of home-schooled students were exceptionally high—the median scores were typically in the 70th to 80th percentile nationally. For example, home-schooled students in grade 3 have a median composite scaled score of 207, which corresponds to the 81st percentile nationwide.[59]

---

[57]Teacher's Union Facts. http://teachersunionexposed.com/protecting.cfm.

[58]"How Lack of Choice Cheats Our Kids Out of a Good Education," John Stossel, 20/20 *ABC News*, January 13, 2006.

[59]Lawrence M. Rudner, "Scholastic Achievement and Demographic Characteristics of Home School Students in 1998. "http://epaa.asu.edu/epaa/v7n8/.

Adjusted for inflation, the cost per student in elementary public schools is about eight times greater than just twenty-five years ago and twenty-five times greater than one hundred years ago.

If government were not in the education business, it seems unlikely that K–12 education would be limited to a brick-and-mortar classroom, one-size-fits-all system, or would even retain those grade designations. The education market is no different from any other market where entrepreneurs and customers come together in numerous and unpredictable ways, and the freer those markets, the more creative and favorable are those ways.

Ironically, the people foisting these programs and policies on us aren't intending to do harm. Yet harm is being done, since causality is not disposed to comport with one's good intentions.

State social planners have repeatedly adopted policies that have resulted in catastrophic human sacrifice and suffering that could have been averted had they only sought out a rudimentary understanding of human nature. History is replete with such disastrous experiments, because those who conducted them refuse to accept the notion that there may be common principles of nature behind each of the preceding disasters.

The thirty million deaths from famine in China following the institution of a collective farming policy is so demonstrative an example of these misguided failures that even the most ardent socialists should, from just this single event, reexamine their understanding of human nature. How many more disasters must social engineers witness before they stop experimenting with human lives and conclude that egalitarian policies designed to promote welfare not only *do not* work, but *can not* and *will not* work?

Problems don't disappear in free markets, of course; they simply are resolved or diminished more efficaciously there than in a system that employs coercion. In free markets, problems invite entrepreneurs to solve them, using solutions that evolve heuristically in an unimaginable variety of ways.

32

THE VIABILITY
OF THE NATION-STATE

WHAT DOES THE FUTURE hold for today's nation-states? Reality will continue to take its toll on central planning and strain the State's ability to control exploding, complex world markets. Innovative entrepreneurs, exploiting communication networks, coupled with human mobility, will play havoc on the continued potency of States. Naturally, States with higher takings and market restrictions will see their most productive citizens and capital gravitate to States with more favorable conditions.[60] Entrepreneurs subject to lower taxes and regulations will gain a competitive advantage over entrepreneurs where such expenses are higher. States with unfavorable business climates will see their labor forces migrating to neighboring States where the business climate has made their labor more valuable to entrepreneurs.

Those States with attractive welfare entitlement programs will be forced to rely increasingly on fiat currency as their source

---

[60]Molly Moore, "Old Money, New Money Flee France and Its Wealth Tax," *Washington Post* Foreign Service, 16 July 2006. On average, at least one millionaire leaves France every day to take up residence in a more wealth-friendly nation, according to a government study.

of funding, since tax increases will only repel those upon whom they rely for their other source of funding. Some States may prohibit their citizens and capital from leaving their jurisdictional borders, but creative minds will discover ways around such obstacles, as they do with all other prohibitions. The day of patriotic State allegiance as a means of keeping the citizenry in line is disappearing.

Eventually, even the most devoted socialists and central planners will lose much of their enthusiasm for pushing utopian ideas when they realize (without actually understanding why) that these ideas only worsen matters for the very people they want to help. Regulations, by their sheer quantity, will become impossible to enforce, and any stigma associated with noncompliance will continue its current trend downward and gradually disappear.

Will the impact of the role of the democratic State as the current exalted master over the lives of people gradually fade, as has the impact of such roles that once were held by monarchs, emperors, and popes? Probably. The residual States may become insignificant pests, unworthy of being extinguished. The decline of the State may be so gradual that, in centuries to come, it will be impossible to mark a date to celebrate the beginning of its decline.

In the meantime, because of the accomplishments of science, markets, and the human spirit, our progress toward better lives will probably continue in spite of the State (provided, of course, that some State doesn't blow us off the planet). And while that progress takes place, most people in today's world will probably continue to attribute the progress to the State. However, such attribution will eventually wane as more realize that, in fact, the State is the greatest hindrance to peace and prosperity.

Today, many may fear a world void of States, but that void is not a void of people. States don't produce—only people do! Teachers educate, engineers build roads, financiers create financial markets, arbiters resolve disputes, guards provide safety, and doctors supply health care; these are very real people. But these same people do not become more brilliant, energetic, efficient, moral, creative, or superhuman at the hands of the State. The facts are overly abundant that the very opposite is engendered in people when at the hands of the State.

In his essay "The Harm That Good Men Do," Bertrand Russell closes with these words:

> Reason may be a small force, but it is constant, and works always in one direction, while the forces of unreason destroy one another in futile strife. Therefore every orgy of unreason in the end strengthens the friends of reason, and shows afresh that they are the only true friends of humanity.[61]

---

[61]Bertrand Russell, "The Harm That Good Men Do," 1926; complete text at http://www005.upp.so-net.ne.jp/russell/0393HGMD.HTM

33

WEALTH IS MORE THAN MATERIAL POSSESSIONS

The highest manifestation of life consists of this: that a being governs its own actions. A thing which is always subject to the direction of another is somewhat of a dead thing.

-Saint Thomas Aquinas (1225–1274)

FOR MOST PEOPLE, WEALTH is far more than money and material possessions. It is love, family, friends, accomplishments, and gaining inner meaning to one's life that trump all that can be bought with the billions of the richest billionaires. Some are born with greater prospects for a good life than others, but where we begin is where we must learn to make our choices to achieve the best life we can from our circumstances. Those who spend their lives engaged in blaming others for their misery will generally continue to experience misery.

Daniel Robinson describes four possibilities for the good life from a philosophical view. They are the *contemplative life* of thought and examination, the *active life* of going out into the world and doing something, the *hedonistic life* of living and enjoying the pleasures of each day, and the *fatalistic life* of accepting every aspect of life as though it were written for us.[62] Undoubtedly, there are many other possibilities for the good life, but no one can dictate the characteristics of that life for another.

In his *A Theory of Justice*, John Rawls argues that State policies should be arranged (*enforced*) so they are always advantageous to the least advantaged group. When he identifies the least advantaged by their economic status, however, he demeans the very essence of life. He demeans the lives of "poor" poets, artists, philosophers, and clerics. He disparages self-accomplishment and becoming oneself. For a poet or a philosopher, money cannot buy self-fulfillment. Often, the financially less advantaged have more rewarding lives than the most financially advantaged. Would a philosopher gain advantage by exchanging his passion for knowledge for the financial holdings of Bill Gates or Michael Jordan? Would John Rawls or Mother Teresa have considered themselves less advantaged than Bill Gates? I suspect not!

---

[62]Daniel Robinson, *The Great Ideas of Philosophy*, 2nd ed., Lecture 50 (The Teaching Company, 2004).

34

THE NATURE OF LIBERTY

Enlightenment is man's emergence from his self-incurred immaturity. For enlightenment of this kind, all that is needed is freedom. And the freedom in question is the most innocuous form of all: freedom to make public use of one's reason in all matters.

-Immanuel Kant (1724–1804)

[T]here is another and greater distinction for which no truly natural or religious reason can be assigned, and that is, the distinction of men into KINGS and SUBJECTS.

-Thomas Paine (1737–1809)

I'VE MAINLY ADDRESSED IN this book the economic benefits of liberty with an eye toward utility and prosperity. Prosperity is the subjective by-product of liberty. Liberty is an end unto itself, with prosperity as its positive externality. A common thread of nature runs through all humanity, but at the same time, each person holds a uniqueness of life that only that individual can master.

Those who claim to be a better master of a life not theirs forfeit a part of their own lives, along with a portion of the lives of those who, wittingly or unwittingly, accept such claims as true. He who believes in a master over his life—be it king, queen, prophet, or statesman—has already forfeited part of the value of living that life. Often, those who accept a master demand that others accept the same master. The value of being a libertarian is that liberty cannot fall prey to those who claim superiority and authority over your life.

Some time ago at a lunch during a Cato Institute seminar, a young libertarian woman at our table asked sadly, "Why are we [libertarians] losing?"

"Why do *you* think we are losing?" I asked her.

"Because the country is getting more socialistic," she responded.

"What would the country look like if you were to win, and what would you be doing when that happened?" She didn't respond. I suspect she hadn't envisioned what it meant to win.

Liberty is not a battle that requires the conversion of others in order to win. Liberty is won when you accept the idea that you are the sole master of your life; when your life is subordinate to none, and no other life is subordinate to yours. When you accept that idea, you are liberated. There will always be those who will claim to be your master, but you will know otherwise. For a libertarian, paying tribute to Caesar may make sense, but believing that tribute is Caesar's due does not!

Liberty is not, as Ronald Reagan suggested, a fragile thing. On the contrary, it is mastery that is fragile; its weakness is evidenced by ubiquitous failures, while the liberty inherent in the human spirit is resilient. Nor does liberty require eternal vigilance, as claimed by Andrew Jackson.

Liberty is a state of mind that does not require the indulgence of others.

35

DISCUSSION POINTS

1. If money grew on trees, would we all be richer?
2. If the rich were poorer, would the poor be richer?
3. Why does liberty bring about prosperity?
4. Is democracy better than freedom?
5. Can morality be taught in public schools?
6. Is there a better guide than the Golden Rule?
7. What do Adam Smith and Charles Darwin have in common?
8. Why is common sense such a powerful tool?
9. Why do we act differently in small groups than in large ones?
10. Why does free health care cost so much?
11. Can compassion be enforced?
12. Do entitlements reduce poverty?
13. What is "the tragedy of the commons"?
14. Why do we care what others believe?
15. Do Michael Jordan and Bill Gates deserve their wealth?
16. Are do-gooders more harmful than evil-doers?
17. Do open borders take away jobs?
18. Can a shorter workweek create more jobs?

19. Who benefits from tariffs?
20. When are communism and liberty compatible?
21. Can socialism work with the right leader?
22. Why do some famish while others feast?
23. Why do underground markets emerge?
24. Who is John Rawls?

INDEX